Divine Guidance

THE LIVING GOD

Mark Walker

**Kingdom
Publishers**

Divine Guidance
The Living God
Copyright© Mark Walker

All Scripture Quotations have been taken from the New International
Version of the Bible.

ISBN: 978-1-913247-95-9

1st Edition by Kingdom Publishers

Kingdom Publishers
London, UK.

You can purchase copies of this book from any leading bookstore or
email **contact@kingdompublishers.co.uk**

Dedication

To all the Greats who have gone before, sacrificing so much in obedience to their Saviour. Their faith conquered kingdoms (Heb.11:33).
To my family, whose love and support mean the world to me.

Acknowledgements

Many thanks to Ken Scott, Ian Darke and Martin Howarth for all their literary advice and to Brian Muir (Air Image) for the excellent photo on the back cover! Every preacher, teacher, leader, youth worker, public speaker etc. should have at least one of those massively thick Systematic Theology books in their libraries. Mine was written by Prof. Wayne Grudem – it's an absolute gem.

Contents

Chapter 1: Guidance through Scripture   11

Chapter 2: Guidance through Others   17

Chapter 3: Guidance through the Holy Spirit   22

Chapter 4: Guidance through Prayer   32

Chapter 5: Guidance through Silence   36

Chapter 6: Guidance through Correction   45

Chapter 7: Next stop – Arequipa!   50

Chapter 8: Step   65

Chapter 9: Gideon's Fleece – the Answer!   72

Chapter 10: TEE – and a Chance Encounter   85

Chapter 11: The Big Day and Beyond   99

Chapter 12: The Journey Continues – a Conclusion   134

CHAPTER 1
Guidance through Scripture

It must be the biggest decision we have to make, or at least up there as one of the biggest. Who am I going to marry? Who am I going to spend the rest of my life with? Who is going to be my sole-mate, my partner through thick and thin, my future wife or husband?

I had come to this point having discovered that the Lord did indeed have someone for me. I was studying at Northumbria Bible College (NBC) in Berwick-upon-Tweed, the most north-eastern town in England. It was a beautiful place to be, with fabulous walks along the banks of the River Tweed and the Cheviot Hills, a range of rolling uplands that straddle the Anglo-Scottish Borders, twinkling in the distance. I was 34 years old, preparing to go to Peru as a missionary with Latin Link. I had reached the stage of not actually wanting a girl-friend – I wanted a wife! What about God though? What did He want? Did He want to use me as a single man? Or had He someone special for me, to work with, to share with to be able to serve with together? I wanted a clear cut answer. I needed to know if I was called to be single or married. So I prayed and fasted and was drawn to a verse in John's gospel. All that week the verse kept ringing in my ears. Then on the Sunday, at a church I had never previously visited, the minister preached on that very verse! Was this purely a coincidence, purely coincidental, or God's incidence? The timing was perfect. I knew the answer. God was speaking to me, communicating His guidance, saying that yes, He did indeed have someone for me!

One of the best ways guidance is provided is through Scripture and the preaching of His Word. The well-known verses of Psalm 16:11, 119:105, 32:8, Proverbs 3:6 and Jeremiah 29:11 come to mind:

You have made known to me the path of life.

Your word is a lamp to my feet and a light for my path.

I will instruct you and teach you in the way you should go; I will counsel you and watch over you.

...in all your ways acknowledge him, and he will make your paths straight.

"For I know the plans I have for you," declares the LORD, "plans to prosper you and not to harm you, plans to give you hope and a future."

How many times have we been guided by a particular verse or passage in the Bible, providing providential leading? How many times have we listened to a sermon and felt that the word was "in season", a message just for me? When I arrived in Ayr, Scotland, in 1988, having been away from the Lord for a number of years, and having just re-committed my life to Him, I visited various churches looking for a spiritual home. The third church happened to be the Baptist church. Pastor McCullins talked about how God used Moses to deliver his people from the hands of the Egyptians. Moses was 80 years old, having spent a long period in Midian in relative inactivity (Ex.2:23). I too had been relatively inactive for the Lord, having spent time away. But not anymore. I could hear God speaking to me clearly, directly, saying that He was going to use me too, that this was to be my church, my new spiritual home. Once again God had answered my prayers and provided guidance through the preaching of His word.

I could not have arrived at a better place. Noel McCullins once shared his desire to serve the Lord as a missionary overseas. It never happened – he was devastated to learn he had been turned down on medical grounds. So instead, he became a Pastor, doing everything possible to send out others. The support I received from the church was phenomenal. It was the perfect place for me. God had guided me to my new spiritual home.

One of our life deacons, Davey Strachan, who is now with the Lord, once shared with me his experiences in the army. He served in 250 Sudan squadron near Cairo, at a time when the enemy where in complete control. The situation was critical for the British army. Every night the bombers would follow the same routine, dropping eight bombs on the airfield, blowing up planes, the runway and the troops. Davey, along with five others, were in a tent, with a dug-out trench readily available outside, to dive into when the planes arrived. The men were petrified. Another Christian colleague took out his pocket Bible and read from John chapter 14, verse 1: *"Do not let your hearts be troubled. Trust in God; trust also in me."* The two men shared about their hope, belief, faith and trust in God, assuring the others that everything would be all right. When the bombers came, the men dived into the ditch, and all six prayed out loud. The bombs dropped very close. They counted them out: "one, two, three, four, five, six, seven." The eighth one never came. "The next day we stepped out the distance between the craters," he told me. "The eighth one would have landed right on top of us." Did the enemy just happen to run out of bombs? Had they, all of a sudden, changed their routine? Did the bomb release mechanism suddenly jam? Davey and his colleagues were in no doubt. They saw the God in whom we can trust, answering their prayers and providing for His children, citing again the words from John 14. They found guidance and encouragement, in a crisis situation, from the word of God. Davey went on to serve the Lord faithfully for the rest of his life. He was a great stalwart, a tremendous man of prayer, a faithful servant who brought enormous blessing to his family, to his church, to his community, to his Lord.

The final year at NBC was challenging, to say the least, particularly with exams looming (five BD's and two from Cambridge, the CDRS). The one exam that bothered me was the BD New Testament Greek. It had a Hebrew option but that quickly went out the window after only two classes! The most difficult part was translating a text into Greek. A list of set texts to study and prepare for was provided, but even with that, there was an enormous amount to cover. For some reason I kept coming back to the passage in Romans, a particularly difficult one to translate, that had come up the previous year.[1] On the evening before the exam, I cried out to the Lord for help, opened up the Bible and read these words:

"Why are you so afraid? Do you still have no faith?" "Look at the birds of the air; they do not sow or reap or store away in barns, and yet your heavenly Father feeds them" (Mk.4:40, Mt.6:26).

"Come to me, all you who are weary and burdened, and I will give you rest" (Mt.11:28).

I am with you; do not be dismayed, for I am your God. I will strengthen you and help you; I will uphold you with my righteous right hand (Is.41:10).

So I handed everything over to Him and went to bed. There was nothing more I could do. And He did give me rest; peace in my heart and a beautiful night's sleep! The next morning, on the way up on the

---

[1] The passage was from Romans 5:12ff. Try reading it in English, never mind translating into Greek!

train to Edinburgh, I read the morning's verse from a daily devotional:

The Lord gave him success in everything he did (Gn.39:3).

What timing! What an encouragement! In the examination room I turned the paper over to commence the exam, and almost whooped for joy; the Romans passage had come up two years in a row! Incredible words of encouragement and guidance from God's word.

In a later scenario, in Arequipa, a Peruvian Pastor also shared from John chapter 14. He too, had been in a very difficult situation requiring enormous faith and belief in God's promises. Pastor Moreno was in the American embassy in Lima, trying to obtain a visa to travel to a Christian conference. He had been encouraged by those wonderful verses in John that seemed to promise so much, verses like John 14:12-14, 15:7, 15:16 and 16:23-24 (*"You may ask me for anything in my name, and I will do it"*). But he was not a man of influence; little money, few contacts, no letters from the bank, the mayor or anyone else of importance to back him up. After the interview, sitting in the processing area, waiting to hear if he had been successful, the person beside him summed up his chances as zero. Roberto took out his Bible and re-read those wonderful promises: *"If you remain in me and my words remain in you, ask whatever you wish, and it will be given you...Then the Father will give you whatever you ask in my name."* He prayed to God saying: "Lord, you have guided me to this place. My chances of success are so slim. But I trust you. I believe in you. Let your will be done." His name was finally called. He had been granted the visa and, incredibly, it was a visa that was valid for ten years! Scripture is indeed the lamp to our feet and the light for out path!

The word of God is living and active, sharper than any double-edged sword. It penetrates deep, deep into our souls to convict, to challenge, to encourage, to guide (Heb.4:12). All Scripture is God-breathed (2Tim.3:16). It is like fire (Jer.23:29). It is the sword of the Spirit (Ef.6:17). It is the living word; active, actual, now-existent, present, alive, breathing. It is so, so powerful, able to bring even the toughest of men to their knees in tears of repentance. It is also one of the ways God speaks to His children. Remember these facts, dear preacher, as you prepare for your next sermon. Pray for great anointing and enablement to speak His word "with great boldness" (Act.4:29). Be like Saul, preaching *"fearlessly in the name of Jesus"* (Act.9:27), asking for prayers to *"fearlessly make known the mystery of the gospel"* (Eph.6:19). Be like *"most of the brothers in the Lord"* who had been *"encouraged to speak the word of God more courageously and fearlessly"* (Ph.1:14). It was God who made David *"bold and stout-hearted"* (Psm.138:3). The righteous are as bold as a lion (Pro.28:1). The word of God is living and active, alive!

So the word of God is our first and foremost way for finding light for our paths. We must always find time each day to immerse ourselves in it, even during the busiest of times. Let's prioritise our quiet-times as a means of soaking in the word of God, of absorbing his divine Presence, of hearing His voice. Let's also prioritise listening to the preaching of His word. God can use others to accomplish His desires through it (Is.55:11). People speak prophetically from God, as they are directed and carried along by the Holy Spirit (2Pet.1:21).

Feeling tired, a little down? Pick up your Bible! Have a big decision to make? Get on your knees! Stop what you are doing. Immerse yourself in Him! When we humble ourselves before God, when we fall down at His feet, when we admit we cannot do it in our own strength, when we cry out to Him, shedding tears of repentance, of sorrow, of love, of joy, when we obey and honour Him in reverent submission (Heb.5:7-9), our prayers are answered. He hears us! Guidance is provided. We serve the living God!

CHAPTER 2
Guidance through Others

So now I knew I was to be married. What was the next big, big question? To whom! Who was it to be? Who was I going to marry? Before I answer that question it is important to note that guidance is not only provided through Scripture and the preaching of the Word, but also through conversation with others.

Of course the greatest person we can have a conversation with is God himself! The Bible contains various examples of this, such as at the burning bush, where detailed instructions were given to Moses to go to Pharaoh and to bring the Israelites out of Egypt (Ex.3:10ff.). Another example is found in Isaiah chapter 6, where the prophet had a powerful vision of the Lord seated on a throne, with seraphs praising the Lord, the doorposts and thresholds shaking and smoke billowing from the temple. Isaiah heard the voice of the Lord speaking directly to him (6:8), again receiving instructions and guidance. In the New Testament there is the example of a light from heaven flashing, then Jesus speaking directly to Paul on the road to Damascus, with instructions to go on to the city. However few of us, as Ken Scott states, will ever experience dramatic events like the aforementioned. God is more likely to use "a combination of factors, a phone call, a sermon, a conversation, a tragedy or a growing inner conviction to lead a person".[2]

---

[2] Ken Scott, 2020: *Anecdotes of an Orcadian, to Peru and Back,* pages 60-61.

At Bible College we often travelled out in teams to take services in the Borders area, in north-east England and Edinburgh. On a visit to the South Bank Mission in Middlesbrough, I spoke to a young man after the service. He was disabled and was praying for guidance about the possibility of going to Bible College. I can't remember speaking to him but he later said that God spoke to him through that conversation in an affirmative way. He was accepted at NBC for one year to see how he got on. John sailed through not only the first year but all three, becoming an inspiration to us all. I take no credit for it, but God was able to use me in that instance, in a sense, as His spokesperson, communicating His message to John.

In 1989, I spent 6 weeks in Cusco, Peru with the Sterkenburgs, a wonderful Dutch missionary family. This was a "Project Timothy" elective, with the emphasis on observing Louis and Ellen in their ministries. They worked extensively with the Quechua Indians, high up in the Andes Mountains, Louis running three Theological Education by Extension (TEE) groups.[3] Towards the end of the stay, I sensed God speaking to me, convicting me. I began to picture myself doing exactly what Louis was doing, working with these hard working *hermanos* and *hermanas*. (On one visit the President of the church urgently had to leave his farm to visit his wife in hospital. Suddenly another *hermano* stood up, asking for volunteers to work his *chakra* - agricultural land. Hands shot up immediately! This was Christianity in action, helping those in times of need).

God was planting seeds in my heart and, on returning to Scotland, the next step was to have a chat with Pastor McCullins, then on to NBC. Missionary societies visited the college on a regular basis and when John Chapman, the International Director of Latin Link came to speak, he made time afterwards to sit down with me. During this

---

[3] We deal with TEE in some detail in chapter 10.

conversation he mentioned something that, I believe, was a prophetic word from the Lord, with regards to my future. It involved a previous conversation he had had with a Quechua Indian. "What is the thing you want most in life brother," John asked him? "Not to be a Quechua Indian," he replied.

I was brought up in Northern Ireland and played rugby for my school in Coleraine. Some of the hardest matches were against the big Belfast schools but we had a great team those years, winning nearly all our games. In my S5 year I was selected as substitute hooker for Ulster schools. In the next year, my final one, I had a magnificent trial, playing really well and hoping to just maybe get promotion onto the first team. But I was not from a Belfast school. I was ignored, overlooked, demoted to third choice and my dreams were shattered, like a glass bauble falling off the Christmas tree, disintegrating into thousands of pieces!

So when John related his conversation, my heart opened to the Quechua people, the most looked down upon people in Peru. In a later scenario, I found myself in the Post Office, waiting to be served. A Quechua man was second in line, when suddenly a white Peruvian pushed in and told him to get to the back. Injustice or what! I spoke up and told him off, half expecting to leave the Post Office with a black eye! But he conceded. The Quechua Indian remained where he was, and justice, in this instance, carried out. Peru's Quechua Indians, descendants of the mighty Inca Empire, are discriminated against on a regular basis. When they move to the cities, many are ashamed to speak their native language. Hence the man's reply to John Chapman's question. Hence my heart opening up to the Quechua people! This was my calling! This was my guidance, through a conversation with a godly man.

In a later scenario in Arequipa, the Pastor of the Quechua church I attended offered me a lift in his taxi. This was a first; I always travelled in a minivan taxi, which was cheap and plentiful. We chatted on the journey down from the shanty town and at the end said our goodbyes. Just as I was leaving, however, he asked a question about tithing which had obviously been on his mind. I felt honoured that he would ask me and it was another half hour before I made it home! He later thanked me for the advice, adding that God had provided the guidance he was seeking.

On another occasion, at a conference, a person shared publicly that she was going through a really difficult period. She shared her doubts, frustrations and feelings of ineffectiveness, as if her ministry was almost worthless. I sensed that I had to speak to her, so after the meeting I just did that. I told her that the Lord had great plans for her; big, big challenges to fulfil and overcome in the future, that her ministry would prosper greatly and flourish in the days to come. She went away greatly encouraged. I would later praise His wonderful name for doing just that; God used her mightily. Her ministry actually went on to benefit thousands of people not only in Peru, but in other Latin American countries as well.

A friend of mine once told me how he received guidance through a letter. He had been changing jobs, (and consequently houses), continuously over a period of time. A good friend wrote saying this was not a good thing to do. It was important for their family to settle down and establish roots in one particular area. My friend felt this was a word from the Lord and did just that.

God can, and often does, provide guidance through others. When you're in tune with God, keep your ears open! Listen to what He is saying. Look out for little "coincidences". At our Bible College open day, I happened to be drinking coffee, standing next to the minister of one of the C of S churches in Jedburgh. It was only natural to engage in conversation which we most certainly did. The result was an invitation to preach in the church at a later date. A link had been established, with the church going on to support us faithfully over the years. I once felt compelled in my sermon preparation to mention giving blood. Lo and behold, after the service at the door, a lady commented that she worked for the Blood Transfusion Service and felt God speaking to her. God spoke to her through that message. The Word of God is living and active! Listen to what other godly people who you respect are saying to you, maybe your parents, pastor, or a friend. God can use any one of us to provide guidance for others, often without us knowing it. Be an encourager! Be a Barnabas (son or daughter of encouragement, Act.4:36). Make a point today of telling someone how precious they are, of how much God loves them. Pray for God to use your words to speak to others. God can use **you** to provide direction and guidance for His people!

CHAPTER 3
Guidance through the Holy Spirit

So now I knew I was to be married. What was the next big question? To who!!! At college I was interested in a student, but her calling was to Africa, mine to Peru. Was this right for us? To take her away from Africa? To forego my calling to Peru? To compromise and go somewhere else? After much prayer, fasting and crying out to the Lord, the answer came in a most unexpected way. I was in my fourth and final year at NBC when a first year student approached saying he had a word from the Lord. He told me that I was going to marry. "Yeah bro', I already know that," I replied. He said: "She is Peruvian. Your future wife is from Peru." Whoa! Whoa! You just know when it is from the Lord. God's timing was perfect, His answer oh so clear. I was not to get involved with the student. My wife to be was thousands of miles away. Praise the Lord! He had answered. I had my guidance through a student who received a word of knowledge or a prophetic word from God.

It should be clearly stated that not all prophecies and words of knowledge are genuine. The Bible warns us to watch out for false prophets, who come in sheep's clothing, but inwardly are ferocious wolves (Mt.7:15, 24:11 etc.). One of my missionary colleagues shares in his book about a similar incident, describing the student as someone "playing God," by declaring so-called "words from God."[4] So we do need to exercise extreme caution when something of this

---

[4] Ken Scott, 2020: *Anecdotes of an Orcadian, to Peru and Back,* p.18.

nature happens. We need to be guided in God's truth (Ps.25:5, 73:24) and by the Holy Spirit (Jn.14:26, 16:13). We need to pray for discernment and wisdom, to be able to distinguish between right and wrong (1Kg.3:9, Ph.1:10). In my case nobody, absolutely nobody, apart from God, knew about my interest in the student. The timing of the word of knowledge was also critical, just when I was committed to a period of intense prayer, praise and fasting, again all done in secret. I also have the gift of discernment, which was a big help as well. I asked God for an answer. I was waiting for a reply. I just didn't expect it to come in such a dramatic way!

Guidance often comes through the work of the Holy Spirit. Jesus himself was sent out into the desert, through the Holy Spirit's leading (Mk.1:12). Both Luke and Matthew refer to Jesus being led by the Spirit:

Jesus, full of the Holy Spirit, returned from the Jordan and was led by the Spirit in the desert (Lk.4:1, Mt.4:1).

In turn, the Holy Spirit is able to lead, guide and direct us (Rom.8:14, Gal.5:18). In some cases, the Spirit makes that direction even clearer by actually speaking directly to the person (I asked the first year student how he knew my wife to be was a Peruvian but he wouldn't tell me). We see this in Acts chapter 8 when Philip meets the Ethiopian eunuch, an important official of Queen Candace. Verse 29 states that the Spirit tells Philip to go to the chariot and stay near it. In Acts 10, something similar happens to Peter. Cornelius, the Roman Centurion, has a vision. An angel of God instructs him to send men to Joppa to bring back Simon Peter. When they arrive, Scripture says that the Spirit told Peter to get up and go with the three men back to Caesarea. The outcome of this was sensational. God was willing to accept men and women from every nation, who fear Him and do what is right (Act.10:35). Jesus came, not only for the Jews, but for all humankind (10:36)! The gift of the Holy Spirit was poured out *"even on the Gentiles"* (10:45-46). Cornelius, his relatives, close friends and a large gathering of people, all received the Holy Spirit. When word spread about what had happened, Peter was severely criticised (11:3). He had to explain precisely what had happened, concluding that he could not stand in God's way (11:17). When the early Jewish Christians heard this, they had no further objections and praised God (11:18).

Later, in the church at Antioch, when the prophets and teachers were worshipping the Lord and fasting, Scripture again states that the Holy Spirit spoke directly to those present, providing instruction, guidance and direction (Acts. 13:2). Barnabas and Saul were to be set apart and sent out by the Holy Spirit on the start of their first great missionary journey (13:4).

On the second of these journeys Paul, along with Silas, went through Syria, Cilicia, Phrygia and Galatia, strengthening the churches (15:40, 16:6). But Luke tells us that they were prevented from preaching in the province of Asia by the Holy Spirit:

When they came to the border of Mysia, they tried to enter Bithynia, but the Spirit of Jesus would not allow them to (16:7).

Again later on, when Paul is on his way to Jerusalem, the Holy Spirit guides him:

"And now, compelled by the Spirit, I am going to Jerusalem, not knowing what will happen to me there. I only know that in every city the Holy Spirit warns me that prison and hardships are facing me" (20:22-23).

How easy it would have been for Paul to listen to the people's pleading to stay and not go on (21:12). But the Holy Spirit had made it very clear to Paul that this was not an option. He had been compelled by the Spirit, or bound in the Spirit, to go to Jerusalem, to suffer for his Lord, to testify to the gospel of God's grace (20:24). He was ready to not only be bound, but also to die for the name of the Lord Jesus (21:13). He considered his life worth nothing in comparison to serving the Lord and to completing his calling (20:24).

We find echoes of these words in Romans 12:1 where we are challenged to offer our bodies as living sacrifices, holy and pleasing to God. This text was actually my very first sermon at Bible College. I can remember nervously rushing through it as fast as possible to get it finished! However, our homiletics teacher would have nothing of the sort:

"You people from Northern Ireland speak far too fast. Slow down and do it again!" (He would later take us to the beach to preach to the sand dunes; perfect training for outdoor evangelism!) Thankfully, it came out better second time round!

In the Old Testament, living sacrifice refers to the animals free from blemish, being presented and devoted to God. Paul is saying that a nobler and more spiritual service is to be rendered – the consecration of ourselves. The sacrifice of a victim was consumed upon the altar and over in a few moments. Our sacrifice is a living and perpetual one, lasting for our entire lives. It is a daily commitment, or should I say, a daily re-commitment.

Those words from Paul remind me so clearly of that disabled brother from the South Bank Mission who came to study at NBC, John Haley. John suffers from cerebral palsy and hydrocephalus, which causes a lack of muscular strength, balance and coordination, as well as headaches, nausea, weakness in the leg, difficulty in focusing, agonizing pain and exhaustion. He was often violently sick and had little control down the whole of the right side. Yet this would not deter him from giving his all for the Lord. One of our outreaches was the hospital service at Berwick Infirmary. A team of 5 students took part every Sunday, collecting the patients from the wards and returning them afterwards. John insisted on doing his fair share and would often lead the service, preach, give his testimony or sing. One day John was leading and it was my turn to preach, so there was an inevitable cross over at the pulpit. It was then I realised just how much this cost John in physical terms. John has given his consent to what I am about to write. It is not pleasant, but it is the only way to sum up his commitment, his love for the Lord at any cost. I could literally smell John's pain. But let me tell you this. He never, ever complained. He always did his part. He loved the Lord with all his heart. He never, ever cried off. To this day we are still best friends. John clearly took Scripture literally, offering his body as a living sacrifice, holy and pleasing to God.

In all of these cases we have seen from the Bible, the Holy Spirit provided direct guidance. In some cases it was through audible words; in others through dreams. The Spirit can also communicate to us through the gifts of prophecy or words of knowledge, or maybe even through strong subjective impressions, convictions, or leadings, when God lays something on our hearts. I had this once when I felt led to bring some money to the church's mid-week prayer meeting. Apart from a free-will offering or a missionary evening, there was never, ever an appeal for money. An unexpected visitor from Africa, not a missionary, shared briefly about himself and I knew the money was to go to him, via the Pastor. Why? I had absolutely no idea. I only knew that I was guided, directed, led, convicted by the Holy Spirit to carry out a certain action, to do a certain thing, and I did just that.

We need to be careful, of course, not to let feelings and emotions control us. There is a danger of placing too much emphasis on subjectivism that, as Grudem puts it, "does not have the controls of Scripture attached to it."[5] On the other hand, as we have seen from the examples quoted from the Bible, we must be open to the living God working in His church today, speaking to us, leading, guiding and communicating to us. He did it in the past and He will do it in the future. We must continually pray "not only that he would keep us from endorsing error, but also that he would keep us from opposing something that is genuinely from him."[6] We must not put out the Spirit's fire, or treat prophecies with contempt. Instead we are to test everything; holding on to the good and avoiding every kind of evil (1Thes.5:19-22).

We must also be open to the gifts of the Spirit, gifts that are *"given for the common good"* (1 Cor.12:7), to strengthen and to edify the church (1Cor.14:26) and indeed to provide guidance. To each one the manifestation of the Spirit is given (1Cor.12:7). To each one, at least one gift is given by the Holy Spirit (1Cor.7:7, 12:11). What is your gift?

When I was in Peru, I noticed how unimportant time was. We had to go to the train station, queue for two or three hours to buy a ticket for a train that was leaving the next day. Inevitably, the next morning, it didn't leave on time! People sit out on the street with their produce from dawn to dusk, trying to make a living. Not here! Time is precious. Time is money and we never have enough of it! But let me make this very clear. God needs your time. He needs you! He needs me. The church, which is His assembly, the congregation of the people of God, the community of God's people, needs us all. We must

---

[5] Wayne Grudem, 1994, *Systematic Theology, an Introduction to Biblical Doctrine, p.* 1042.
[6] So Grudem, 1994, p.1042.

all come together and work together for the glory of God. We must all do our part, every single one of us. Peter writes in 1Pet.4:10:

Each one should use whatever gift he has received to serve others, faithfully administrating God's grace in its various forms.

We all have different gifts, according to Romans chapter 12:6-8. Here we find gifts that are mainly associated with natural abilities, such as serving, teaching, encouraging, contributing to the needs of others, showing mercy and leadership. Within this listing, quite an assortment and array of gifts could be included. For example, the gift of serving could include those who help with car parking, uplifting the offering, preparing for communion, helping in the kitchen, playing the guitar, etc. There is almost an interminable list of things to do in the church and community, so many opportunities for people to get involved. One of the signs of a healthy church, in my opinion, is one that does just that – involving as many as possible in serving one and another which, in turn, is serving the Lord. When these things are all done in His name, dedicated to His kingdom and empowered by the Holy Spirit, the church is strengthened and edified and God is glorified. The body performs as one unit. Everyone feels they are doing their part.

Then there are the gifts related to the miraculous, such as prophecy, healing, miracles, tongues, and distinguishing between spirits. God has blessed the church with an amazing variety of spiritual gifts. A healthy church will have a great variation of gifts. Paul makes it quite clear, when referring to the body as a single unit made up of many parts, that *"each one of us is a part of it"* with a role to play, contributing to the overall function (1 Cor.12:12-26). The foot is as important as the hand, the ear as the eye. Those parts of the body that seem to be weaker are indispensable!

In the Inca Empire, *chasquis* were used to deliver messages, gifts and products. Each *chasqui* ran up to 240 kilometres a day, along the coast from Nazca to Tumbes and high up into the Andes Mountains, along roads, trails and rope bridges, finally arriving at the capital, Cusco. Rest points, or change over stations, called *tambos* were established. As the *chasqui* approached the relay station, he would blow his *pututu,* a conch shell used as a trumpet, to alert the next runner to get ready for the hand over.[7] Can you imagine the reaction of the exhausted runner if he found the *tambo* empty, if the next *chasqui* was not there to do his part? He would have no alternative but to struggle on as best he could, plodding on another 240 kilometres to the next change over point, at a considerably reduced pace. The whole efficiency of the system would have been reduced, all because one person did not do their part, did not contribute, did not turn up.

At my best friend's wedding in Derbyshire, the reception was held in the church hall, directly underneath the sanctuary. The bride looked glorious in a fabulous, white dress. A meal had been prepared and everything went according to plan. As people were starting to head home, I noticed the minister who had conducted the service, stacking the chairs and tables away, all on his own. Well, in my eyes, that did not sit well, so I stripped off the jacket and tie and for the next twenty minutes helped him tidy up, sweep the floor and finally lock the building. I asked him, where were the other helpers? Why did he have to tidy up on his own? "I'm afraid we can't afford a caretaker," was his reply. But I wasn't referring to a caretaker. I was referring to those members of the church who had no doubt fully enjoyed the buffet and all the other festivities before rushing off, leaving the poor man all on his own.

---

[7] Wikipedia (Chasqui) Also based on Pete Foley's excellent chapel talk at NBC.

Harry Hopkins was the 8th Secretary of Commerce and President Roosevelt's closest personal advisor during World War 2. (He came to be known as the "Deputy President"). Sadly, due to stomach cancer, his health was not good. Wendell Wilkie, when visiting the White House, asked the President why he placed such faith in Hopkins. Roosevelt told him that if he ever became President, "you'll learn what a lonely job this is, and you'll discover the need for someone like Harry Hopkins who asks for nothing except to serve you."[8] That was why he was in the White House. This thin, sickly, almost nondescript person, was the President's right hand man. He was there not to receive or get something from the President, but instead to give his all in total service and commitment.

Every one of us is needed to do our part. We depend on each other. We need each other. The church can only function properly when we all chip in, when we all contribute. It can be a sacrifice. It requires a lot of time and effort. But by doing so, we are offering our bodies as living sacrifices, holy and pleasing to God.

Are you using your gift for His glory, to serve Him and to bless others? Maybe you have recently been asked to serve on a particular church committee. Maybe the leaders have recognised your gift and are asking for help with a specific role or ministry. Are you willing to offer your body as a living sacrifice to God? Are you willing to give your all for Him? Are you willing to serve Him? During these difficult times, we need an outpouring of the Holy Spirit like never before. Pray for just that. Pray for discernment. Pray for wisdom. Pray for visions and dreams. Pray for protection from misinterpretation and from endorsing error. We need more of the Spirit's leading today. We too need to hear that divine voice speaking

---

[8] HistoryNet.com (Harry Hopkins).

to us, guiding us, compelling us. We need to hear His voice and to reply, just like Samuel:

"Speak, LORD, for your servant is listening" (1Sam.3:9-18).

CHAPTER 4
Guidance through Prayer

Someone once said that prayer is the place where burdens change shoulders. We all know how powerful and essential prayer is (Jam.5:16). It is our direct link with the Father, part of that wonderful personal relationship we have with the living, Lord God Almighty. Even Jesus offered up prayers and petitions with loud cries and tears (Heb.5:7).

Prayer helps us to cope with difficult situations. We have all, no doubt, had to cry out to Him, asking for help, in times of need. We also pray to ask for forgiveness, confessing our sins, to praise and thank the Lord and to reconfirm our trust and dependence. We also pray for guidance and direction.

The need to pray for just this occurred when I was travelling into Peru's remote Amazon jungle to a place I had never been to before. It was a two day trek to get to a small town called Kiteni, firstly by train to Quillabamba and then seven hours further in on a dirt road. I had no idea how to find out what time the bus departed, where it left from, even if it went every day. I was quite worried about the situation and prayed for guidance, for help, for direction. Lo and behold, who should be sitting opposite me on the train but the wife of the President of the local evangelical church in Quillabamba! I had never met her before then, but something made me talk to her at some point in the eight hour journey. She was able to give me all the information I needed and later took me to the exact spot where the bus was due to depart from. As she was travelling further on, in another direction, she was also able to recommend a restaurant where the food was good and the local coffee, as fresh from the plantations as you could get, literally sensational, bursting with flavour! What must the locals have thought as they heard the "oohs" and "ahhs" of this strange gringo, as he ordered cup after cup of delicious Peruvian coffee! God is good! He loves it when we show our childlike trust, crying out to Him in prayer.

Nehemiah worked for King Artaxerxes as a favoured servant, a cupbearer or wine steward. He must have been a rather jovial character, as he had never previously appeared sad or down in the King's presence. Nehemiah went on to explain that his sadness was rooted in the fact that Jerusalem, the city where his fathers were buried, lay in ruins. The King asked him what he wanted. In a brief moment before answering, Nehemiah prayed to God, probably for, among other things, inspiration and guidance (Neh.2:1-5). This passage is the perfect example of an "arrow", or "bullet" prayer; a quick, short, almost a cry for help, in moments of indecision and need. Just as the arrow flies swiftly and straight to its target, so do our prayers to God. They are shot up to heaven, in an instant, in a single breath, taking seconds to both arrive and for God to give an answer.

I once had a "chance" encounter in Arequipa with a Peruvian colleague. We bumped into each other outside the post office; the colleague was in Arequipa getting some documents updated, I was there to collect the mail. He was in quite a panic as the officials were requesting more documentation which would have required further travelling. We both did the only thing possible – sending up arrow prayers to God, asking for help. I continued praying for the situation as my colleague went back in. He returned with a massive smile on his face! Our prayers had been answered; the documents approved!

In another instance, I was travelling with a Peruvian colleague on a remote mountain road, to a village called Chumbivilcas, high up in the Andes. You've got to understand that we're talking about 1997, when satellite navigation was unheard of, at least in the *Sierra*,[9] and road signs non-existent. The directions we had been given never mentioned this Y junction, two roads to choose from, only one leading in the right direction. What would you do? Toss a coin? Pray? Of course, like me, you would choose the latter and send an arrow prayer up to heaven. Then an amazing thing happened. Here, out in the back of beyond, where it was extremely rare to meet another vehicle yet alone another soul, we came across two workers repairing the road! They were able to give us the directions needed to arrive safely to our destination. A swift prayer, an instant answer! Prayer is powerful! Prayer works!

We made it to Chumbivilcas, receiving an incredibly warm welcome and fabulous hospitality. Approximately sixty people crowded in to the small, tiny church that night to hear God's word. This was followed by a huge meal which was so kind and generous of our hosts, but, due to the altitude which slows down digestion, resulted in little sleep!

I doubt if you'll ever find yourself at a Y junction, high up in the remote Andes. But there will definitely be times in your life when you will need to shoot off arrow prayers to heaven, seeking guidance and direction in a particular situation. Don't be afraid to do just that, to involve God in the decision making process, to cry out for help in your moment of need.

---

[9] Spanish word used to describe the highlands of Peru, which are named after the "saw" like shape of some of the mountain ranges.

Can I encourage you also to think about forming a prayer triplet/quadruplet group, if you don't belong to one already? I meet monthly for lunch and prayer (Covid permitting) with friends David Craig, Chris Groves and Alan Telfer. We take it turn about to host the meeting and provide lunch. The fellowship over the years has been amazing and we have all, at some time or other, shared very personal points for prayer. Sometimes these have been arrow prayers, as a text is received with a prayer request. Never, ever underestimate the power of prayer. Remember the words of our Saviour in Mark's gospel:

I tell you the truth, if anyone says to this mountain, "Go, throw yourself into the sea," and does not doubt in his heart but believes that what he says will happen, it will be done for him. Therefore I tell you, whatever you ask for in prayer, believe that you have received it, and it will be yours. Mk.11:23-24

CHAPTER 5

Guidance through Silence

The corona virus has been a nightmare for just about everyone, everywhere. We have all been affected by it in some form or other. So many loved ones have been lost. So many businesses have had to close, with the consequent loss of jobs. We have experienced restrictions on travel, lockdowns and, in some countries, curfews. Many are struggling financially, emotionally, mentally, even spiritually.

Yet there have been some benefits from these dreadful times with, for many, the pace of life slowing down, resulting in less rushing around. Walking has become even more popular, as has gardening, cycling, jogging, reading, knitting, painting by numbers, even jig-saw puzzling! For me, I was able to spend time in the garden, attacking all the weeds that had grown out of control. I actually made a new friend, a beautiful blackbird, who just happened to appear at weeding time, when the slater insects and worms were uprooted! As a family, we were also able to enjoy some of the beautiful walks close to our house. There was one hill in particular, discovered by chance, which offered up fabulous views of the Irish Sea, the beautiful Isle of Arran and Aisla Craig (also known as "Paddy's milestone", possibly due to the immigrants from Ireland who used the tiny volcanic isle as a marking point, indicating their near arrival in Scotland. It is a fabulous seabird sanctuary, home to gannets and puffins. The rare "blue hone" micro-granite is used to make curling stones; next time you watch the curling competition in the Winter Olympics, be aware that every single curling stone, from every country taking part, is made from Aisla Craig granite)!

When restrictions permitted, we also visited the seaside town of St Andrews, famous for its many golf courses (known worldwide as "The Home of Golf"), beautiful beaches and University. It was a joy to explore the medieval centre of narrow alleys, cobbled streets and ancient ruins. It was also a delight to visit the nearby fishing villages of St Monans, Pittenweem and Anstruther. The Fife coastal path, which links these celebrated East Neuk villages, provided more opportunities to enjoy the incredible world our God has created. The day culminated with a visit to one of the most beautiful spots in this area, the village of Crial.

The Bible tells us in Psalm 46:10 to *"be still, and know that I am God."* We don't know who wrote these words of wisdom but the writer was really on the ball, summing up life perfectly. Sometimes it is good to be still. Sometimes, even when we're having a bad day, full of problems and things going wrong, it is good to slow down, pause and turn to God. And you know something, that's easier said that it sounds. It's not a natural thing for many of us to do. We like to be active, rushing around doing this, doing that, trying to instantly solve the problem. We like to be in control at all times. And when that doesn't happen, we're lost, almost in despair. Sometimes it's really important to just stop trying to do it on our own, getting worked up, frustrated, angry. Just be still, come before the Lord on bended knee, and hand the problem over to Him.

Just like David did, a man who had many difficulties in his life, in one instance being hunted down and almost killed by Saul; in another, pretending insanity to stay alive.

Those poignant words of Psalm 23, verse 4 come to mind: *"Even though I walk through the valley of the shadow of death, I will fear no evil, for you are with me; your rod and your staff, they comfort me."* He also wrote the following:

Be still before the LORD and wait patiently for him... Psm. 37:7.

...I have stilled and quietened my soul; like a weaned child with its mother, like a weaned child is my soul within me... put your hope in the LORD both now and for evermore Psm. 131:2-3.

He had learned not to let the noise, the intense pressure, the stress, the almost unsolvable problems of life, keep him from communing with God, from hearing the voice of God, from receiving the comfort, the reassurance, the touch, the blessings, the guidance and the empowering of his heavenly father. He had learned effectively to say: "I can't do it. I can't cope. But I know you can, and I'm handing it over to you."

Just like Jesus had to do. Luke chapter 4 tells us that Jesus was in Capernaum, having just taught in the synagogue, having just healed both a man possessed by a demon and Simon's mother-in-law. Then, when the sun was setting, at the end of a busy day, *"...the people brought to Jesus all who had various kinds of sickness, and laying his hands on each one, he healed them"* (verse 40). Mark adds that the whole town gathered at the door, including all the sick and demon-possessed, and that many were healed (1:32-34)! Luke adds:

Moreover, demons came out of many people, shouting, "You are the Son of God!" But he rebuked them and would not allow them to speak, because they knew he was the Christ (4:41).

What a busy, exhausting, confrontational, energy-sapping day! What did Jesus do? Did he have a lie-in? Did he have a rest? No! Very early the next morning, while it was still dark, he went off to a solitary place to pray (Mk.1:35). He had to meet with the Father, to commune with him, to be still, renewed and strengthened. And in these quiet times, in these times of solitude and prayer, guidance was given. When Simon and his companions found him, Jesus announced a change of plans. It was time to move on, to go and preach in the nearby villages and throughout Galilee (Mk.1:36-39). Even during His busiest times, Jesus made a point of seeking out places of solitude to pray, to converse and to be still.

What about us? Our goal in life should be to be like Christ, all the time. John writes the following:

Whoever claims to live in him must walk as Jesus did (1Jn.2:6).

Paul tells us that we are being *"transformed into his likeness with ever-increasing glory," "conformed to the likeness of his Son"* (2 Cor.3:18; Rom.8:29). We are to be imitators of God (Ef.5:1). Peter tells us, admittedly with regards to suffering, that we should follow the example of Christ and walk in his steps (1Pet.2:21).

When life becomes impossible for us, when we feel under so much pressure, when we've had a busy, exhausting, confrontational, energy-sapping day, we too need to find a solitary place where we won't be disturbed. We too need to find time to meet with God, to commune with the Father, to pray. How does the saying go: a problem shared is a problem halved, a burden shared is half a burden? The Bible tells us that for sustenance and support, we are to cast our cares and anxieties on the Lord (Ps.55:22; 1Pet.5:7). We are to, in effect, hand the problem over to Him, transferring our heavy burdens onto His strong shoulders, into His mighty hands.

This time of stillness will renew our strength – physically, mentally, emotionally and spiritually. This time of stillness will empower us to overcome, will clarify our minds, helping us to unscramble our thoughts, to see the way ahead, to find a solution, a way out. It will also help us to know God's guidance and will for our lives, to hear His voice speaking to us, through the Holy Spirit, through Scripture. Just as the Lord spoke to Elijah; not in the great and powerful wind that tore the mountain apart and shattered the rocks, not in the earthquake, not in the fire, but in the gentle whisper. And with that whisper came the guidance and encouragement Elijah needed, instructions to go to the Desert of Damascus to anoint Hazael, Jehu and Elisha (1Ki.19:11-18). What preacher hasn't heard that whisper in the middle of the night, with an idea on their mind, quickly jotting it down on a piece of paper before returning to bed? Even in the stillness of sleep, we can hear from God via sudden inspirations. As the prophet Isaiah writes, *"Whether you turn to the right or to the left, your ears will hear a voice behind you, saying, this is the way; walk in it" (30:21).*

Martin Haworth in his book "A Clearing of the Mists," notes the importance of listening to God, with reference to Isaiah 50:4-5:

The Sovereign Lord has given me an instructed tongue, to know the word that sustains the weary. He wakens me morning by morning, wakens my ear to listen like one being taught. The Sovereign Lord has opened my ears, and I have not been rebellious; I have not drawn back.

He advises us to "note the attitude of waiting and listening first so that we may be instructed in what to say and what to do. Because of the servant's love for and dependence upon God, the servant rises early as well as consistently to have undisturbed time to relate to God...When we bring the concerns of our lives, our loved ones and all those God has placed around us into the quiet place, God can direct by giving us a burden for someone and often along with that the clarity of what we should say or do."[10]

Sadly, earthquakes are a common occurrence in many parts of the world. In May 2013 a severe quake struck Bangladesh, resulting in death and destruction. Miraculously a woman was rescued after being entombed underground for 17 days. Despite all the sophisticated sound equipment used to detect the faintest of noises, such as seismic sensors and acoustic listening devices, the rescuers relied on something else – total silence. When the heavy machines were shut down, when everyone remained quiet, the sensors were able to pick up the tiny, exhausted voice of the lady buried below, and eventually bring her back up safely. When we turn all our "machines" off, when we quieten our hearts before the Lord, we too will hear that still, small voice, that gentle whisper, calling to us.

This time of stillness will also benefit us spiritually, helping us to grow in Christian maturity, resisting sin and being conformed more and more to His will. It helps us to focus on our spiritual side, which in turn, provides the physical strength to overcome. Our spirits are lifted up and replenished or, as Romans 8:10 puts it, our spirit *"is alive."* Being still helps us to live a life overflowing with love, joy, peace, patience, kindness, goodness, faithfulness, gentleness and self-control (Gal.5:22-23). This helps us to grow more like Christ, cultivating more of the fruits of the spirit in us; more holiness, more Christ like characteristics. When this happens, we experience true love, true joy, true goodness, true happiness and true peace in our lives.

Being still involves a time of yielding to God, sitting in the stillness of His presence, focusing our entire being on Him, filling our mind with

---

[10] Martin Haworth, 2016, *A Clearing of the Mists,* pp. 156-57.

God and His truth (cf. Rom. 12:2). Paul exhorts us to do just that, thinking about whatever is true, noble, lovely, admirable, excellent and praiseworthy (Ph. 4:8). We need to fully absorb the incredible significances, depths and meanings of the promises of God. They have the power to transform us from people who are burdened, overcome, weighed down and depressed, into a people of hope, light, power and energy! We need to meditate on God's word (Jos. 1:8; Psm. 1:2, 119:97), on His precepts (Psm. 119:15, 78), on His decrees (Psm. 119:23, 49), on His statutes (Psm. 119:99) and on His promises (Psm. 119:148). We need to imbibe both the incredible love He has for us (Psm. 48:9) and His omnipotence (Psm. 77:12, 119:27, 145:5). We need to spend quality time deliberately focusing on God's goodness to us and bringing ourselves to a state of rest, to a time of sitting with God in His presence, slowing down, being still and knowing Him. This is sacred time, when we feel His closeness, coming before Him in quietness and trust. Allow your heart, soul and inner being to feel gratitude for His grace and love. Allow the knowledge of such overwhelming love to cover you, to penetrate deep into your souls and spirits. Breathe in His goodness, breathe out self criticism. Breathe in His love, breathe out your tension and worries. Meditate on His wonderful promises such as:

"I will be with you; I will never leave you nor forsake you. Be strong and courageous ...Do not be terrified; do not be discouraged, for the LORD your God will be with you wherever you go" (Jos. 1:5-9).

"...I know the plans I have for you...plans to prosper you and not to harm you, plans to give you hope and a future" (Jer. 29:11).

"I have chosen you...I am with you...I am your God...I will strengthen you and help you; I will uphold you with my righteous right hand...For I am the LORD, your God, who takes hold of your

right hand and says to you, Do not fear; I will help you...I myself will help you" (Is.41:9-14).

When we slowly read, prayerfully imbibe and humbly rely upon what God has revealed to us in His word, our minds are renewed, our spirits uplifted, our confidence and faith restored. Meditation is a conscious, continuous engagement of the mind with God. It is part of the process by which Scripture penetrates our innermost being with a divine touch of His presence, with the light of illumination and the transforming power of the Holy Spirit. Meditation, as we have seen, is Biblical, heightening our spiritual and mental alertness and the sense of God's presence, as we focus less on material things and worldly activities, and more on eternal spiritual realities. In our busy, busy non-stop world, we need to take time-out to be still and know God, experiencing that inner peace (Ph.4:7). We need to focus on specific Bible passages, even memorising them if we can, deeply reflecting on their meaning. God loves it when we want to spend time with him, when we allow our hearts to feel gratitude for His grace and love. Soak in His presence. Live in His peace. Imagine Jesus is actually present, walking by your side. You have nothing to fear. Say to yourself: "He is with me, He is with me now." "He will strengthen and help me." "I am not alone." Forget about your worries, hardships, anxieties, pains, deadlines. Take courage from the promise that He knows our every need, our wants, our desires, our aspirations, our sufferings, our failings. He hears us. He knows us. He helps us. He loves us. He forgives us. He protects, encourages and provides for us. He holds us in the palm of his hand (Is.49:15-16).

In our moments of need, we have someone to cry out to, to help us through, someone to transfer our heavy burdens to, strong shoulders to lean on. By gazing at Him, we gain His perspective on our lives. This time alone is essential for unscrambling our thoughts and soothing out the day ahead, energising us and empowering us. Enjoy His presence. Focus on it. Sit down and be quiet! Relax in this precious time together. Ask for His stillness to stay with you. Allow it to wash over you. Ask for His tangible presence to move with you to face the day ahead. Feel how wonderful it is to say His name, to sing praises to Him! Feel His closeness, closer even than the air we breathe! Feel His touch! He is the First and the Last...the living One. ..alive for ever and ever (Rev.1:17-18)!

"Be still, and know that I am God."

CHAPTER 6
Guidance through Correction

In 1911, in Armagh, Northern Ireland, Thomas J Walker, my granddad, opened a drapery store. This expanded over the years, to include ladies fashions, menswear, children's wear and household goods. In the 1950's, my Dad took over the running of the store, and, together with Mum, enlarged and modernised it. The business prospered greatly until its closure in February 2014, after over a century's trading, when Mervyn and Ivy retired.

With this background, it was no surprise that I too went into business, opening a gift shop in Ayr on 3rd July, 1988. In those early days, I decided to rent a stall at Ayr's annual Flower Show, in an attempt to generate more sales. It meant a lot of extra work, carting merchandise from the shop, to the car, to the show. As the council provided a stack of black bin bags for uplifting the rubbish, it was only natural to use these to transport the stock. So that's what I did, filling the bags from the stock room, bringing them down to the alley, opening the side door ready for transportation. Suddenly I remembered something else was needed from upstairs, so it was back up to the stock room, quickly fish out the stuff and return down to the alley. Only to find the black bags gone! When I looked out onto the street, I discovered the culprit – the bin lorry! Just at that time, at that very precise moment, they came by to collect the rubbish! Just when I'd nipped upstairs for a few seconds, the men came and threw all the sacks into the lorry! It was too late to do anything. The stock was unusable.

God's word is divided into two testaments, the old and the new. Scripture refers, in the same way, to two covenants, the old covenant and the new. The old covenant is associated with specific requirements and promises; Leviticus 26 stating clearly that there are rewards for obedience and punishment for disobedience (cf.Psm.91). Sadly, the Hebrews often chose the latter.

What about the new covenant? In the new covenant, Jesus came to die for our sins, *"the righteous for the unrighteous, to bring you to God"* (1Pet.3:18). This is the *"good news of great joy"* of the Gospel (Lk.2:10). Through Jesus, we have been reconciled to God, having been justified by His blood (Rom.5:9-10). We have been born again of the Spirit of God (Jn.3:5-8). Jesus Christ, *"the Righteous One,"* is the atoning sacrifice for our sins (1Jn.2:1-2). We have crossed over from death to life (Jn.5:24). He has rescued us from the dominion of darkness and brought us into the kingdom of God (Col.1:13-14). We have been redeemed. Our sins are forgiven. And because of all these wonderful acts of salvation, the Bible describes us as the children of God, the people of God (1Jn.3:1, Psm.144:15). His divine presence lives within us (1Cor.6:19). We have this wonderful personal relational with the all powerful, Lord God Almighty. Good news or what!

That is the divine part. But we have our part to play as well. We are required to have faith. We are also required to be obedient and to *"obey his commands"* (1Jn.2:3-6, 3:22, 24, 5:3; 2Jn.6; Jn.14:15-24, 15:10; Rev.12:17). We are to do as He says, putting His words into practise (Lk.6:46-49). We must walk as Jesus did.

I don't know about you, but there have been times, as a Christian, when I have fallen short of this and not been obedient to God, when I have struggled with sin, when the old self has taken over (Rom.6:6), when sin has reigned, forcing me to obey its evil desires (Rom.6:12). One such time was that day at the Flower Show when the bin lorry just happened to appear at the very moment I nipped upstairs. Was this purely a coincidence, or just rotten bad luck? Nothing of the sort! Right at that moment, as the stock was being squashed to pulp, I knew that God was speaking to me. He let me know that my disobedience was unacceptable and that, in a sense, my own actions had caused this to happen. I had not been obeying His commands, remaining in His love, pleasing Him, living close to Him, walking in obedience to Him. God had to communicate to me to let me know that this was totally unacceptable. That much more was expected from a child of the holy, living, Lord God Almighty, that I had to repent, to change my ways, to recommit to Him once again. And that was exactly what I did. I cried out for forgiveness, the peace of God came upon me, and I was spiritually strengthened, able to resist the devil and battle on.

Sometimes things happen to us to buck us up, to correct us. Sometimes, like disobedient children, we need correction (Heb.12:7). I believe, most sincerely, that God can, in certain circumstances, make things happen in order to communicate His disapproval, His displeasure, His disappointment in His children (Pro.3:12). God has called us to live holy and honourable lives that are pleasing to Him (1Thes.4:3-7). It is His will that we should learn to control our bodies, being disciplined and self-controlled (1Pet.1:13f.), not conforming to the evil desires we once had. We are called to be holy in all we do, for it is written: *"Be holy, because I am holy"* (Lev.11; 1Pet.1:16). We are called to live our *"lives as strangers here in reverent fear"* (1Pet.1:17), offering our bodies as living sacrifices, holy and pleasing to God (Rom. 12:1). We are called to live holy and godly lives and to make every effort to be found spotless, blameless and at peace with him (2Pet. 3:11-14).

I heard a fabulous analogy one day on a Christian radio station. It referred to two dogs and how the one that was well fed became stronger, while the other one, who didn't receive food, became weaker. We must do everything to avoid the temptation to sin. On the one hand, we need to feed ourselves spiritually, through prayer and quiet times, reading God's word; through praise and worship, through communion with God and with His people, walking close to Him, calling out to Him, soaking up His presence, walking in the light, the light of life (Jn. 8:12). On the other hand, we need to starve the temptation to sin; to restrict and control our time on the TV, perhaps on the Internet, or whatever tempts us. The one you feed becomes stronger. The one you don't feed becomes weaker. We need to feed ourselves spiritually. The Holy Spirit enables us to live lives free of continual sin, with the ability to overcome the pressures and temptations of the world. This does not mean that we will have perfect lives and live as saints. It does mean, however, that the pattern of life will not be one of continuing indulgence to sin. We must refrain from a life pattern of continual sin.

I hope you're living in a close relationship with our Lord just now, walking in obedience to Him. I hope you have no "idols" in your life. I hope you do not let sin reign in your mortal body so that you obey its evil desires. I hope sin is not your master (Rom. 6:12-14). If things are going wrong in your life, maybe it is a sign of God's displeasure. Maybe he is speaking to you, expressing this displeasure through the circumstances of correction. It is not pleasant. But you can get through it. Remember, as born again children of God, we have died to sin and been raised to a new life (Rom. 6:1-4). Our old self has been *"crucified with him so that the body of sin might be done away with, that we should no longer be slaves to sin – because anyone who has died has been freed from sin"* (Rom.6:6-7). By the amazing grace of God, through His incredible love and forgiveness, we have been forgiven and set free from sin. We have become *"slaves to righteousness...slaves to God"* (Rom.6:18-23), which leads to holiness, goodness and purity.

Remember also that the one who is in you, is greater than the one who is in the world (1Jn.4:4). The Holy Spirit is so, so powerful! He will help you, as Scripture clearly states: *"Everyone born of God overcomes the world"* (1Jn.5:4). He who has the Son has life (1Jn.5:12). *"Anyone born of God does not continue to sin...God keeps him safe, and the evil one cannot harm him"* (1Jn.5:18). He will bring peace in your life (Rom.8:6). The wonderful promises of God! Take them on board. Absorb them. Breathe them in. Live by them. Go forward in hope, in strength, in confidence and power. You can do it! With God all things are possible (Mt.19:26). Nothing is impossible with God (Lk.18:27).

CHAPTER 7
Next stop, Arequipa!

Very early in the morning, in the summer of 1993, I said my goodbyes to Mum and Dad at Ayr train station, en-route for Glasgow, then London, then Peru. I felt like a snow flake lost in the ocean, unsure of the future, uncertain of what lay ahead, tiny, insignificant, scared, and vulnerable. I was going away for three and a half years. Despite the sun trying to poke its head out of the pearl, grey dawn, I felt cold inside. Cold, nervous, fearful; leaving loved ones behind; stepping out into the unknown; giving up my business, my family, my church, my home; into a new culture, a new continent, a new challenge. Then the words of the Psalmist came to mind:

If I rise on the wings of the dawn, if I settle on the far side of the sea, even there your hand will guide me, your right hand will hold me fast (Psm.139:9-10).

On the long journey down to London, I took my Bible out and read and meditated on these wonderful words, along with Psalm 37:23-24, 63:8 and Isaiah 41:13. Yes, I was so small and vulnerable, almost helpless. But I was not alone. God's hand was upon me, guiding me, holding me, protecting me, providing stability, support and strength.

Two images from my sporting background came to mind. The first one involved a Scottish rugby international, Steve Munro. Steve was recovering from an injury, gradually working his way back into the Ayr first team. Hence his appearance for our team, the seconds. I cannot describe the difference his presence made to the morale of our team. To have a Scottish international taking the warm up, playing along-side us, offering words of wisdom, advice and encouragement. It was just awesome! Any fear of the opposition dissipated. An international rugby player was on our team. Steve was on our side.

And what about the opposition? As soon as they realised who they were up against, their faces dropped! Fear set in. They were petrified. Needless to say, we won the match easily that day! Suddenly, I realised that I too was not alone on this fearful journey into the unknown. The Lord God Almighty, creator of the world, maker of the universe, the great, sovereign, supreme, all powerful, all knowing, all seeing, King of kings and Lord of lords, was with me every step of the way. Scripture describes him as being our "light," our "tower," "shield," "rock," "fortress," a horn of strength." He's our refuge, our loving heavenly Father who we can turn to for help in our moments of need. He goes before us. He knows everything – our wants, our desires, our inspirations, even the number of hairs on our heads (which in my case isn't too many)! He listens to us. He helps us. He provides for us. He protects us. He encourages us. He opens doors for us. He closes doors and prevents us going down the wrong path. He loves his children intensely, even more than parents doted on their offspring. He adores us. He blesses us. He is here to cry out to in our moments of need, to help us through difficult times. We are not alone. *"I am your God,"* writes the prophet Isaiah in chapter 41, verses 10-14. *"I am with you...I will strengthen you and help you...I will uphold you with my righteous right hand."* I am on your side! A wide smile spread across my face as the reality sank in. Whatever difficulties and problems lay ahead, they were nothing to worry about. Every one of them would be overcome. God was with me. He was on my side.

The smile widened further as the second image came to mind. As a youngster I loved all kinds of sports, including water skiing. Every weekend in the summer we would be out skiing on two skies, one ski, trick skies, jump skies, a disk, a chair on top of a disk...anything went! So it was no surprise when I ended up one summer in the United States at Buna camp, as a water ski instructor. We taught kids from as young as 5 years old, how to ski. The technique was quite simple. An instructor would ski alongside the girl or boy, and, with one hand, literally lift them out of the water, their skies dangling all over the place. Eventually, when the skies were pointing in the right direction, the instructor lowered the child gently on to the water with a firm hand on their shoulder. *"Don't you dare let go off me!"* was a common enough cry! But we already had and the young boy or girl was skiing by themselves. Then, the inevitable happened. They began to doubt, to wonder, and to disbelieve. They would turn their heads, look across at the instructor, find no hand on their shoulder and fall into the water! God's hand is always upon us. He never, ever takes it away. He has his grip firmly on our shoulders. The powerful, mighty hand of God supports and strengthens us. He upholds us with His righteous right hand. Through the topsy-turvy of life, with all its ups and downs, bumps and knocks along the way, He never removes that stabling, supportive hand – the true hand of God! Herein lies our strength. Herein lies our security and confidence. He is with us. He is the LORD, our God.

The words of Alfred Smith's wonderful hymn came to mind, followed by Jenny Hewer's:

I do not know what lies ahead, the way I cannot see; yet One stands near to be my guide, He'll show the way to me: I know who holds the future, and He'll guide me with His hand; with God things just don't happen, everything by Him is planned. So as I face tomorrow, with its problems large and small, I'll trust the God of miracles, give to Him my all.

Father, I place into your hands the things that I can't do. Father, I place into your hands the times that I've been through. Father, I place into your hands the way that I should go, for I know I always can trust You.

In the heat of the carriage, bound for London, the little lamb slept peacefully, safe in the arms of the loving Father (Is.40:11).

I arrived in Lima on the 24th September 1993, together with Doctor John and Paula Jameson and family, stopping briefly in the capital for documentation and work visas. It was then on to Arequipa for language study and cultural orientation. Arequipa is a beautiful city, 2286 metres (over 7,500 feet), above sea level. It is situated at the foot of an ice-capped volcano called *El Misti,* 5821 metres above sea level and thankfully dormant! It is known as the "white city," as many of its colonial buildings are made out of white ashlar or *sillar,* a volcanic stone extracted from *El Misti* or the two other neighbouring volcanoes, *Chanchani* and *Pichu Pichu.* The city is renowned for its beautiful historical centre, a UNESCO World Cultural Heritage listing. It is also renowned for having one of the most pleasant settings and climates in Peru, with a mean average temperature before sundown of 23 degrees centigrade. The sun shines on 360 days of the year! I wrote in one of my prayer letters:

We've had our annual rainfall already in March and don't expect to see any more till the new year. A tough missionary location!

Part of the cultural adaptation involved living in situ with a Peruvian family. Latin Link's long serving missionaries, Rosemary Gibson and Ruth Green, organised the programme. The plan was to spend the first 3 months in a *pueblo joven* (shanty town), in Alto Cayma, high up in the city's hills, before moving to another family to allow for further cultural learning experience. As none of the family members spoke English, these placements were ideal for studying at language school in the morning, before returning home to put the theory into practice, in a wonderful home environment.

Latin Link has a school in Arequipa, called the *Colegio Internacional*, which is held in extremely high esteem in the local community, with ethics and values based on biblical Christian principles. One of the security personnel at the school was Dionicio, who, along with his wife Berta, had graduated from a Bible College in Lima. They kindly agreed to take me in to their family on a *pensión* basis, with the mission paying for food and accommodation. The other family members, at the time, consisted of Eli (16), Rubén (14), Matt (5), along with Berta's sister Martha, 2 dogs, 6 rabbits, 8 little rabbits and now me! Peruvians are some of the hardest workers I have ever met, often having more than one job, not only to make ends meet, but also to improve their lot and push themselves forward. So although things were quite basic at the time, and we only had an outside yard tap for our water supply, Alto Cayma has now developed into a beautiful neighbourhood, with all the mod-cons.

Once a week, I would visit the home of an incredible missionary couple from Sheffield, whose two kids had been born and raised in Peru. It was so good to be able to talk English again and to catch up on all the footie news. Their pastoral support and love helped me through a difficult time because I found language learning rather frustrating and mentally exhausting. Okay, some people, like my Greek lecturer at NBC, (who decided to learn the Czech language during the summer holidays!), are natural linguists and find learning a new language no problem whatsoever. But for others, it is not as easy. At Bible college, everyone talked about "culture shock," arriving in a different country miles away from home, experiencing a new culture, a new environment, a new way of life.[11] However, modern Peruvian, and indeed South American culture in general, is amazing! You do have to be very careful of thieving, but generally speaking, the people are amazing, the scenery stunning, the food incredible and the culture and history totally absorbing.[12] No, the problem for me was not the culture. The problem was not being able to interact and participate in that culture. This is particularly difficult for "professionals" like me, a business person used to making decisions and being in control.

Language learning is a long, slow, frustrating process, requiring enormous perseverance and stamina. You are brought back to your early childhood, being able to say a few words and phrases, hopefully progressing each day, expanding on the never ending vocabulary, practising the pronunciation, the vowels, the grammar, the home work, day after day after day. It is intensive mental work, with the mind often remaining active in the early evening, making it hard to get a good night's rest. It would be nice to wake up fresh and rested and "raring to go" each morning. Sadly, that did not happen often. (I wish the Australian spin bowler, Peter Sleep's, nickname could have applied to me – "sounda"!). But little by little, with the Lord's help, through prayer and the prayers of others, through persisting, persevering and battling on, progress was made.

After the three months with Dionicio, Berta and the kids (and animals!) I moved to live with a new family, Javier, Betty, their son Favio and 3 dogs. Favio was around my age and turned out to be a

---

[11] On Home Leave Assignment, at NBC, I mentioned the frustrations I experienced during the language learning process. After the meeting two students, whose first language was not English, thanked me for sharing this; they were experiencing the exact same thing!

[12] I mention modern day culture, which is distinct from days gone by when things were a lot different: lack of medical facilities, food shortages, limited electricity, poor toilet facilities, underdeveloped infrastructure, social unrest and persecution. Any of these things would inevitably have been an enormous shock to the system for many of us, myself included.

good friend and companion. Their daughter, Beatriz, was actually studying at Methody College Belfast, on an exchange programme from the *Colegio Internacional,* so Mum and Dad were able to return some of the excellent hospitality I was receiving by taking her out for the week end and bringing some "goodies" for a special treat.

Again, I was welcomed with open arms as one of the family. Their friendship, love, encouragement and support helped me enormously to adapt to this amazing culture. Here is an example of a typical day in my life in June 1994:

3am: Yawn! These Peruvian dogs haven't half got strong vocal cords. Thankfully our 3 are dozing contentedly. Must join them...

6am: Yawn! Time to rise and open the curtains. Another sunny morning. Quiet time to start the day. Better practise my vowels as well as the vocab, and the homework...

7am: Breakfast with Javier. Betty has made lovely fresh pineapple juice, a boiled egg, bread, jam and hot milk – is he spoiled or what? Better get moving. "Micro" bus arrives. It's inevitably packed but they stop for us anyway. Squeeze in, there's heaps of room! Still, it's only the equivalent of 13 pence for the 25 minute ride to language school. "Baja"!, I say in crisp, early morning Spanish. "BAJA"! Shouting always helps here! It finally stops.

7.45am: Bible study to start our day at school. We all take it in turns to give a short word in Spanish, if possible. Time for classes – "practice your vowels Marcos, practise your vowels". "I do Teach, I do".

12.30pm: Home again. There's a market close by. The bicycle vendors are common here. So are the microphones that adorn them. "Bananas, lovely bananas, 3p each" is blasted out. Not bad though, avocados at 15p, cucumbers 8p, oranges and apples 9p, spuds 25p per kilo. How does that compare to your prices!

1pm: Lunch time. Betty's out working at Latin Link's school, which has around 1,300 pupils. Javier is an economist and works flexi time, hence he's here with me. Good opportunity to chat. Man, how does he handle that hot, spicy sauce! Food's good – so is the company.

2.30pm: Tutor arrives to the house for 1½ hours communication skills. We talk about all sorts of things, even visit the shops together. Quite fun really.

4.15pm: Coffee break, read the paper from home. Blues are in the FA cup final I see – surely we can't beat the mighty reds again! A little more study and homework, then time for the BBC's World Service sports desk.

6pm: Tea time – light affair due to the altitude.

6.30pm: If it's Tuesday, it's off to a meeting of our Latin Link personnel; Thursday – my Church's mid-week Bible study. If nothing else on, there's always vocab to be learned or perhaps a "relaxing" read of something in Spanish.

8pm: Now I can really relax – it's English now! Time to settle down for the evening; read, listen to music, pray and praise. It's been a good day really. Yawn! It's nice and quiet at the moment – something must be amiss. No, they're starting up again – man's best friends? Still, one gets used to it. And, all truth told, I love it. Prayer to end off the day..."Thank you Father for bringing me to such a great country..."

10.30pm: Just time to pop my head out of the window and look down at our 3 dozing below. "Nite girls, sleep well". A face peeps out of the kennel, looks up and winks. "You too pal" she says! I hope so.

As at Bible College, I was encouraged to visit different churches and denominations. I settled into a modern Spanish speaking church in the centre of Arequipa for the morning service. In the afternoons, I alternated between 4 smaller Quechua churches on the outskirts of the city. The great thing about South American churches is that they are full of young people, all of whom have either Spanish or Portuguese as their first language. So while parts of the services were in Quechua, particularly the beautiful hymns, Spanish would inevitably be spoken as well. Incidentally, the original plan was to start Quechua studies in Arequipa as well, but the mission's Peru Executive correctly thought it would be best to postpone this until the start of my second term. Otherwise, I would have returned to the UK for Home Leave Assignment with two languages and little opportunity to practise either.

Anyway, I thoroughly enjoyed visiting the Quechua churches, which provided excellent opportunities for participation; sharing greetings, giving my testimony, even singing! It was great to eventually accept their invitations to preach, although it had to initially be read out word for word. I was also able to take part in door to door visitation in the local area of *San Martín*. One lady had just lost her brother and was deeply upset. It was a pure coincidence, she told us, that she was in her house, just at the exact time we called. She invited us in to talk, to share wonderful words of encouragement from Scripture and to pray for her. It was such a joy for our group when she gave her life to the Lord.

As the months passed, my involvement with the Quechua church grew. The Evangelical Church of Peru (IEP) is one of the country's largest Quechua speaking denominations. Missionaries have always worked in partnership, alongside our Peruvian Pastors, colleagues and leaders, providing assistance wherever possible. Enormous credit is due to those who have gone before, Peruvians and missionaries alike who often experienced opposition and even persecution. They endured extreme hardships and difficult living conditions.

Part of the continued training involved trips into the mountains to conventions and retreats. One such journey was to Santa Lucia. Again my September 1994 prayer letter tells the story:

A Weekend in St Lucia

Hmm, Santa Lucia actually, not quite that idyllic island in the Caribbean! Still, in my eyes, it was just as romantic – 4572 metres (15,000 feet) high up in the Andean mountains; fresh, crisp mountain air; ever so friendly people (many who had travelled on foot, horse, bicycle etc. to be here), fresh meat for lunch each day – alpaca; being part of the Quechua community. No tour could better this – eat your heart out St Lucia!

Yet I wasn't here as a tourist. This was part of my continuing cultural adaptation, a wonderful opportunity to observe, take part where possible and to experience once again living amongst our Quechua brothers and sisters – a real privilege indeed. Folks had gathered together from Quechua churches far and wide, for a weekend convention; a time to renew old friendships, to make plans for the future and come together to hear God's word and worship His name.

*The community spirit was excellent. We ate together – lots of soups, meat, rice and spuds, washed down with hot, sweet coffee. We slept together – two to a bed (we were the guests after all!); many on the floors sleeping on llama skins, heaps of blankets etc. (I wore three pairs of trousers, two pairs of socks, three shirts, a thick coat and hat – **in bed** – and was still cold! Tried to wash my teeth in the morning only to find the river had frozen solid!)*

We worshipped together – lots of lovely Quechua music, the men playing guitars and mandolins, the ladies singing hymns of praise. And we worked together. I'd come as part of an all Peruvian team, including the President of the IEP in Arequipa, who ably ministered the Word on Sunday and took discipleship groups on the Saturday. Another member of the team had brought a small generator, with colour TV and video – quite a novelty in a place where there was no electricity. We ended the evening, wrapped up and cuddled together, watching Christian videos. And Marcos? Well I was able to give my usual greetings and share testimony during the Sunday services. For me, it was what I received from them – their love and kindness, their warmth and fellowship, their support and encouragement. Travelling back along the dark, bumpy mountain roads, singing songs along the way, it felt good to be here; to belong, to be accepted, to be used by God. It reminded me of a devotional reading about a person carrying a lantern on a dark road at night who sees only one step ahead. When one takes that step, the lamp moves forward and another step is made clear. Eventually, the destination is reached. Perhaps these were my initial steps into the unknown, steps that would lead, for certain, to a final destination.

BIBLE TEACHING

I had qualified from Bible College with a BD from the University of London. While this doesn't make you a teacher, it did help to provide opportunities to lecture in the various theological Institutions in Peru. But before that happened, the Executive wisely suggested further orientation and arranged firstly a three week placement with Alex and Giovanna Donnelly in Trujillo in the north, followed by five days at the Evangelical Seminary in Lima with Barry and Anthea Harrison. These visits gave invaluable insights into different teaching techniques, many of which I would adopt in the days ahead.

In fact, it was in January 1995, when I first went to teach at a Bible Institute in Ayaviri, 3658 metres (12,000 feet), high up in the Andes Mountains. The town is actually located not far from Lake Titicaca, the world's highest navigable body of water and home to the famous *Islas Uros,* the manmade islands constructed from *totora* reeds. My colleague and I decided to take the cheap twenty minute flight to Juliaca, returning by overnight bus. Although we were at the airport in good time, with our bags checked in, the plane, for some unexplained reason, decided to leave ten minutes early – with our luggage, but without us! Fortunately, there was another one four hours later which actually did leave on time!

Anyway, it proved to be a most valuable and rewarding three weeks. Apart from my classes, I was asked to preach each Sunday in different locations, pray for six new benches for the Ayaviri church, give a short word at a wedding anniversary and attend a Youth Convention, an Elders retreat and a funeral! Two of the Sundays were spent in the *alturas* (high mountains) at Ocuviri (5am rise to catch a lorry) and Nuñoa (3am to get a bus).

Ayaviri was followed by our team conference, held in the Scripture Union campsite at Kawai, close to Lima. It was good to be back at sea level, listening to the waves crashing in to the sandy beach. It was also good to have a concentrated period of listening to God's word, singing His praises and coming together in prayer and fellowship, a bit like Spring Harvest and Keswick, though with business sessions thrown in as well. I soon discovered a tall tower with fabulous views of the sea on one side and the hills on the other. It was to become my little sanctuary, a place to go to during the day and at night for a time of quietness, meditation, prayer, and talking to the Lord (which is prayer anyway)!

The only drawback were the wretched mozzies! The accommodation blocks were all supposedly mozzie free, with netting on the windows. Those clever little beasties (thankfully not malaria carrying), would somehow find a way in, wait till you were almost asleep, then creep up and buzz in your ear to check if dinner was ready. A hand would come up to swipe them away. Half an hour later, in a deep sleep, no hand appeared and they tucked in for supper! I have this theory that the blood in the human body is, in time, able to change to make it unattractive to our little friends. I think this happened on the very last night when I finally got a good night's sleep!

Another highlight was the "specials" evening, a time for folk to show their talents through drama, singing or whatever. I particularly enjoyed the year when we were asked to make the presentation representative of our home countries. It was a fabulous multi-national event as we had folk from all over the world. I managed to sing a lovely Irish melody called *The Boys from County Armagh*. The secret was to get everyone to sing along in the chorus, the words of which are quite apt:

It's my old Irish home, far across the foam.

Although I've often left it, in foreign lands to roam.

No matter where I wander, through cities near or far,

Sure, my heart's at home in old Ireland, in the County of Armagh.

I hadn't planned it, but when they all started swaying from side to side in perfect rhythm, I knew it had been a success!

Next stop was Andahuaylas. Our missionary there was yet another of those incredibly dedicated people who gave their whole lives to the ministry – Cherry Noble. Again, our mission has a long history of working with the IEP in that area.[13] I taught an introductory course entitled "Abundant Life" at the Bible Institute in nearby Talavera, which gave me a lot of scope to branch out at various points, expanding on certain themes. I was also asked to teach an extra course on "How to Illustrate Sermons and Talks." One of the methods Jesus used to teach was, of course, through the use of parables, using examples and language from everyday scenarios. It was a powerful tool to grasp the listener's attention and reinforce the teaching. I had noticed a distinct lack of illustrations in the sermons so set about correcting this. Half way through one of the lectures I decided to lighten things somewhat, with a touch of drama. I had once seen a movie where a young couple displayed their faith in each other by falling back into each other's arms, one at a time! So I invited a volunteer up to the front and got him to fall backwards, leaving it to the last possible minute to catch him (don't do this at home; maybe in the swimming pool)! Then he did the same for me!

---

[13] Latin Link was formed when the Regions Beyond Missionary Union (RBMU) and the Evangelical Union of South America (EUSA) amalgamated. Both RBMU and EUSA had missionaries in Andahuaylas.

Believe me when I say, it requires considerable faith and belief in the person behind you! (And who is the Person who is always behind us)!

If I can digress slightly, I also noticed a lack of facial expression in the singing of hymns and choruses in most parts I visited. Or maybe a glum, miserable, sad face does count as expression. But when you're singing the equivalent in Spanish of "I'm so glad that Jesus loves me"? Come on. I once helped organise a retreat for the students and staff from the Chiguata Bible Institute, just outside Arequipa. We hired a bus and ended up at the SIM campsite, not far from the sea. The facilities were excellent with a large hall for times of devotion and praise and lots of external activities including a swimming pool, archery, and the inevitable football pitches. I had never seen such expressions of joy and happiness on their faces!

Perhaps the highlight was a weekend visit to the *campo,* a two hours journey by minibus, followed by two hours on foot. We visited nearly all the houses in the village and were delighted to see two families return to the fold at the next day's service. I was asked to preach at the early morning elder's meeting which started at 6am!

My time in Arequipa, for now, was drawing to an end. Cusco was beckoning! I was scheduled to move to my new base on the 1st September 1995. Before that, however, I had to return unexpectedly to Andahuaylas.

CHAPTER 8
Step

Latin Link has a wonderful programme called Step. We were one of the first missions to offer mainly young people, the opportunity to experience cross-cultural encounters at first hand and, at the same time, serve the local church or community in a very practical way.[14] The Steppers are able to share God's love in a very tangible way as they live and work alongside the local people, offering their support and encouragement through practical and community based projects.

The *Sierra* is a fabulous location for Step, for a number of reasons. Over the years the tourist industry has changed in Peru. Much more emphasis is placed now on eco-tourism; many companies taking the tourists into the local communities to experience the indigenous way of life; life style, food, crafts, culture etc. That, of course, for me was one of the joys of serving the Lord in the *Sierra*. My work and ministry involved doing just that, spending time in these wonderful farming communities, sharing the Word of God as well as offering support, encouragement and fellowship to each other. The Steppers were particularly good at this, forming very close bonds within the local communities they visited.

---

[14] The mission is also at the forefront of multi-directional mission, sending and receiving personnel both to and from Latin America. Most members serve in Central and South America, but a growing number are coming from Latin America to serve in Britain and Ireland and elsewhere in Europe.

On the practical side, each team is allocated a certain amount of money to go towards the building and construction work. The local *hermanos* often pay them in kind, providing free accommodation and food donations. They also provide skilled craftsmen to work alongside the team, with many of the young people from the local churches also chipping in. And it is inevitable, come Sunday, members of the team will be asked to not only participate in the Church services, but to preach God's word. What an opportunity for our young people! How often do they get such an opportunity like this in their own churches back home? In many places they might never be asked to take part in the services let alone preach! Not so here. As there are always members of the team who act as translators, the whole team can be involved, preparing songs, testimonies, readings, prayers and messages. I can remember the first time I had to lead the service in my home church. Was I nervous? Incredibly so! Did I doubt my own ability? Goes without saying! Did it bring me closer to God? So, so much closer, as I had to cry out for help, for support, for empowering. Many of the Steppers experience similar feelings and are amazed at how God has used them. Many go on to take a step further, becoming full time Christian workers.

Earth quakes are common occurrences in Peru as the country is located in a seismic zone, with the Nazca and South American tectonic plates constantly moving. The Incas actually employed construction techniques that resemble anti-seismic design features, as anyone who has visited Machu Picchu can testify (the walls are built at an angle, with the stones reducing in size as the building progresses upwards). Cusco experienced several devastating quakes in 1650, 1950 and 1986. On the 13th January, 1998, a smaller quake struck in the remote jungle region of Yanatile. Due to the powerful tremors, a dam's wall collapsed, resulting in severe flooding and a huge mud and boulder slide. Five villages were affected, leaving eleven people dead with many homes and *chakras* ruined. Four Evangelical churches were destroyed. On the 27th February, a second landslide engulfed the other nearby valley in Santa Teresa, this time with approximately fifteen fatalities. The village, including the local church, was completely covered with mud and boulders. Peru's President flew in by helicopter bringing aid and promising financial support. He had to come by helicopter because, at that time, the only way in was by train to Aguas Calientes, the station that serves Machu Picchu, then on by mule or foot, deep into the jungle. One of the government's promises was to build a road in to the area via another route. In December of that year, Dr. Nat Davies and I, after an eight hour drive from Cusco, found ourselves on that very road. We reached a point, approximately three hours walk from Santa Teresa, where the road literally ran out! Day by day, the excavators were creeping ever closer to the village. But they still had some way to go.

We were met by some of the local *hermanos,* who were on hand to carry the Bibles and medicines, and to escort us to the village. One part was particularly dicey, traversing across a steep rock face, where a slip on the crevice would result in almost certain death. The *hermanos* crossed over without hesitation. I managed to do the same, though certainly not at their speed! Nat was harnessed across. A dislodged rock roared past, disappearing from sight like a shooting star in the night sky – here one moment, gone the next! Thankfully, that did not apply to us!

Eventually we reached the village, sweating and exhausted having been up, down and around hills and mountains! We stayed in the home of the church President, experiencing some fabulous hospitality – freshly picked fruit from the plantations, locally grown *yuca* (root plant similar to the potato), delicious *caldos* (soups fortified with potatoes, vegetables, meat) and tasted again some of the best coffee in the world, the beans literally picked from the bushes that surrounded us! But we were here to access the possibility of sending in a Step team, to help rebuild two churches, and soon got down to work. Where would the new churches be built? Where would the team be housed and fed? Were there local skilled builders available to work with the Steppers? Were the buildings to made out of *adobes* (mud/straw "bricks," hardened in the sun), or concrete bricks? What was the budget? The list went on and on, but we did give the project our backing on one condition – that the road was completed. We felt, very strongly, on medical grounds, that there had to be direct access to Santa Teresa.

The road was completed, and in July 1999 a team, supervised by Rosemary Flack, arrived to build the two churches in Santa Teresa and Yanatile. What an experience for them – no TV (no electricity), mozzies at night, early to bed, the lads sleeping in a "tent" made out of corrugated iron sheeting, eating the occasional *cuy* (guinea pig), two hours hike from Santa Teresa to Yanatile, no post for weeks, cravings for jam and cakes...! Yet despite all these inconveniences, they helped to not only rebuild the two churches, but to rekindle the faith and hope of the local Christians, who had suffered so much. The Steppers blended in to the two communities, taking the children to their hearts, participating in all the temporary church services and leaving behind memories that will last forever. They deserved their well earned rest; a four day hike on the Inca trail to Machu Picchu!

Many more Step teams would arrive in the future, equally as committed to the incredible work they do in construction, evangelism, working with young folk and children and so much more. A team helped to construct a beautiful new classroom in the Sicuani Bible Institute. Another helped in the Zarzuela church in Cusco. Everywhere they go, they leave behind their indelible mark on the churches and communities they serve. Well done everyone!

Anyway, I am getting a bit ahead of myself. In the summer of 1995, Cherry Noble had to return suddenly to the UK. Sadly, her Mum was not well and she had to return at short notice. Cherry had organised a Step team to come to Andahuaylas in August to work alongside the *hermanos,* in the construction of various buildings as part of a refuge centre for elderly people. As I had already taught in Andahuaylas, and knew the proposed site, the Executive asked me to meet the team and help them settle in. Hence my arrival, a little ahead of them, to make sure everything was at hand. I was warmly welcomed into the home of the local Pastor, Isaías and Olga Calle, and their son Oliver. The next day a group of young people gathered to prepare food for a fund raising event for the refuge centre. They were making a delicious looking chocolate cake. I decided to get a closer look and sat down in front of the most beautiful girl I had ever seen! She was busy putting the chocolate icing on top of the huge cake and didn't seem to notice me. But I noticed her! Her beautiful long hair. Those gorgeous brown eyes. The pure olive skin. That smile – yes, I had just been caught stirring! Her name was Violeta Alarcón Altamirano, and, as one would have it, or rather, as God had planned it, she was heavily involved with the project. Our paths crossed regularly. The bemused Steppers missed nothing and "coincidentally," Violeta and I were placed together at the joint lunch when all the workers from the local churches, and the Steppers, sat down together. I was falling in love! Was Violeta God's choice for me? Was I God's choice for her? I would have plenty of time to mull this over and to pray in the days ahead. The team were scheduled to spend six weeks on the project, but I had a house move to make, and had to return to Arequipa to prepare for my departure to Cusco.

On Friday 1st September, I arrived in Cusco with all my belongings. I was returning to the former capital of the Incas for the first time since my stay with the Sterkenburgs in 1989. My new abode was a lovely bungalow beside a very dedicated Welsh couple, Nat and Doreen Davies in the *Magisterio* district of the city. Another one of those, almost thirty years of service missionaries, had recently arrived from working in Juliaca to join this new team, the aforementioned Rosemary Flack, a nurse from Farnham, England. Under Nat and Doreen's leadership, we soon blended into a wonderfully supportive group, meeting regularly for prayer, praise, chat and maybe the odd cup of tea!

However, there was still the question of the Step team and a certain lady called Violeta! I returned to Andahuaylas to check up on them both! The team was progressing well on the bungalow as well as helping in the construction of other buildings. As usual, they made quite an impact in the local community, and were asked to do a broadcast on local radio. As usual, they continued in their role as matchmakers, presenting me with a thank you gift of a mock engagement ring!

As the time approached for my departure, I just had to pay a visit to a certain lady's house, to see her, talk to her, and spend time alone together. Her younger sister, Carmen, answered the door and I was shown to a small settee while she went to fetch Violeta. Her Dad popped his head in to say "*¡Hola!*" – cripes! Then Vio appeared on her own, looking as stunning as ever, and came and sat on the little settee beside me, very, very close! I knew the feeling was mutual! We chatted; Carmen returned with a soft drink and biscuit, and I returned to Cusco.

Was this the girl I had been waiting for? Was this the person to be my future wife, as promised by God at Bible College? This was one of the biggest decisions I had to make in my life. And I didn't want to get it wrong. So as usual, in times like this, I turned to prayer, to fasting, to seeking His guidance and direction. This was massive. I had to get it right; to find my partner in life, to find someone to share everything with, someone who loved the Lord and wanted to serve Him. I was drawn to those famous verses in Ecclesiastes chapter four:

Two are better than one, because they have a good return for their work...A cord of three strands is not quickly broken (v.9-12).

Our future had to be in God's hands. We had to have His blessing, His confirmation, His approval. This was big! What was His answer going to be?

CHAPTER 9

Gideon's Fleece – the Answer!

We all have Bible heroes and one of mine is definitely Gideon. The people in his day regarded him as no one special, a rather ordinary, nondescript character, certainly not someone to be anointed and used powerfully by God. He came from the weakest clan in Israel. Not only that, but he was, in his own words, the least in the family (Jdg.6:15).

Yet in the eyes of God, there is no such thing as an insignificant person. William Carey is the perfect example of this. In human terms, he didn't appear to be the right person to go as a missionary to India, where the people are mainly Buddhist. He had never studied at Bible College and was a balding man with sensitive skin; how was he going to cope with the extreme heat? But he had heard God's call and off he went. He became one of the most respected and arguably successful missionaries India has ever seen, becoming a great linguist, spending 41 years translating the entire Bible into Bengali. The "Father of Modern Missions," as he became known, founded the Serampore College and University, the first degree awarding University in India, as well as setting up medical institutions in different places. He even had a stamp issued by the Hindu government in his honour! He "retired" from his work in India to work as a Pastor in Leicestershire. An "insignificant" character used so mightily and powerfully by God.[15]

Scripture highlights perfectly the amazing dichotomy that really should exist between the all powerful, immense, holy God and little sinful old me. Of course, the reason why it doesn't exist is due to the *"good news of great joy"* I've already mentioned, the people we have become through the blood of Jesus and the wonderful, personal relationship we have with God the Father. Scripture also shows clearly, time and time again, how God can use ordinary people to do extraordinary things. He can use any one of us to do great things for Him. We don't have to be rich and famous, attractive and appealing, big and strong, an out and out extrovert, for God to be able to use us. We must never doubt, or under estimate, our usefulness to God. We must never let feelings of inferiority get us down. He can enable and empower us to perform way beyond our natural abilities. With His anointing, with His presence (Jdg.6:12, 16), with His promises (7:7, 9), with Him on our side (7:14-15, 22), anything is possible! In God's hands, He can make it happen. Any obstacle can be overcome (Ph.4:13)!

And what an obstacle the Israelites had to overcome. Their situation was dire. For seven years the oppressive power of Midian had run supreme. In fact, it was so oppressive that the Israelites had to abandon their homes, their crops and their livestock and flee to the mountain clefts, to the caves and to their strongholds. They abandoned everything in an attempt to save their lives (Jdg.6:2). The Midianites were like *"swarms of locusts. It was impossible to count the men and their camels... Their camels could no more be counted than the sand on the seashore"* (Jdg.6:5, 7:12). Against such a powerful, mighty army, God chose Gideon. And He used him

---

[15] Wikipedia (William Carey); Bethany Global University (William Carey).

mightily. The Lord called him to a task that required immense courage and leadership. God chose unimpressive Gideon, calling him a "mighty warrior" (6:12). Gideon never dreamed of leading Israel to a military victory over their enemies. But that's exactly what he did. Things were going to be different this time. It was time to face up to their "mountain" and to overcome it.

In such a situation, Gideon had every right to ask for confirmation (6:17, 39)! The odds, in the world's eyes, were heavily stacked against him. The main sign was to be a woollen fleece. If the next morning there was dew only on the fleece, but not on the ground, it would confirm God's calling (6:37). The next day he rose early, squeezed the fleece and wrung out a bowlful of water! For further confirmation, he requested that this time the fleece should be dry, with the ground around it covered with dew. Scripture tells us that *That night God did so. Only the fleece was dry; all the ground was covered with dew"* (6:40).

Note how personal the fleece is; the conditions drawn up by Gideon and God alone. It is a private affair, a test involving only God and Gideon. Note also Gideon's faith and total belief in God. He didn't doubt God could do it. Even when later, when God told him to reduce the number of troops (so the Israelites could not boast about their own strength), he gladly obeyed. First down to 10,000, then 300! Three hundred troops against an army that was so large it appeared to be as thick as locusts. Three hundred against a vast, enormous army, so large that it was impossible to count (6:5)! You got to be joking. These odds are insuperable. No one, in their right mind, would take them on. But God encouraged Gideon by allowing him to listen in to what the Midianites were saying. The enemy themselves believed God had already given the whole camp into Gideon's hands (7:14)! Gideon worshipped God. He praised God's name. He believed wholeheartedly in the Lord God Almighty. He obeyed, and when the

300 men blew their trumpets and broke the jars in their hands and shouted "A sword for the LORD and for Gideon!" the Midianites panicked and fled. The Lord caused the men throughout the camp to turn on each other with their swords and the whole army fled! Israel had won! The mighty warrior had triumphed! God was victorious!

It is not often mentioned, but there are, in my opinion, other examples of "fleeces" in Scripture, such as in 1Sam.14:8f. Once again the people of Israel were in dire straits. This time the Philistines were the dominant force, with a mighty army consisting of at least three thousand chariots, six thousand charioteers and soldiers as numerous as the sand on the seashore (1Sam.13:5). Again the men of Israel panicked, hiding in caves, thickets, among the rocks and in pits and cisterns (v.6). All of them "were quaking with fear" (v.7), which is perhaps understandable as none of them, with the exception of Saul and Jonathan, had a sword or spear to fight with (v.19-22). Jonathan, Saul's son, along with his young armour-bearer, in a moment of incredible bravery and faith, decided to cross over along a pass to a Philistine outpost to "test the water." The plan was to deliberately let the enemy see them, then listen carefully to their reaction. If they said "Wait there until we come to you," Jonathan and his armour bearer would remain where they were. But if they said: "Come up to us," they would climb up and take them on (v.8-10). This was to be their sign that the Lord had given the enemy into their hands. The odds were not in their favour either. How could two young men take on an outpost that was backed up by such a powerful army, the mighty Philistines? The answer is, of course, that they were not alone, that God was with them, on their side, acting on their behalf (14:6). In the first attack, Jonathan and his armour-bearer killed some twenty men (v.14). Then a panic, sent by God, struck the whole of the Philistine army. The ground shook. The vast army, in total confusion, melted away, running in all directions, striking each other down (v.16-22). The unimaginable had happened; that vast, vast army, whose soldiers were uncountable, as numerous as the sand on the seashore, had been routed. As Jonathan had previously stated: "Nothing can hinder the Lord from saving, whether by many or by few" (v.6). And by few the Lord did just that, rescuing His people, intervening miraculously on their behalf once again (v.23).

The final "fleece" I want to look at is found in Genesis, chapter twenty four. In this instance, Abraham is looking for a wife for his son Isaac, not someone local from Canaan, but rather one of their own relatives, from their own clan (24:4, 40). And so he sent his chief servant off on this rather difficult mission. How was the servant to know who to pick? As I've said earlier, it must be one of the biggest decisions we ever have to make, finding the right person to share our lives with. So how was the servant to know? What was he going to do? Firstly, he came to the Lord in prayer, asking for a successful outcome (24:12, 45). Secondly he, like Abraham, had incredible faith, believing that God would send an angel to lead him on the right path and to make his journey a success (v.7, 40, 48). And thirdly, when he arrived at a well on the outskirts of Nahor, he prayed again, asking for certain, specific words to be said which would be confirmation of God's will and approval. Before he had even finished praying, Rebekah, the granddaughter of Abraham's brother, appeared and spoke those exact words. The chief servant immediately bowed down and worshipped the Lord (v.48). He knew the Lord had guided him to this place. He knew the Lord had chosen Rebekah to be Isaac's wife (v.44). Leban, Rebekah's brother, and Bethuel, her mum, after hearing what had happened, concluded that:

This is from the LORD; we can say nothing to you one way or the other. Here is Rebekah; take her and go, and let her become the wife of your master's son, as the LORD has directed (24:50-51).

I felt that my relationship with God at the time was so profound, so personal, so intimate, and so close, that I too could ask for divine guidance in this way. Isaac was looking for a wife, so was I. For Abraham, it was so important to find the right person. Likewise for me, this was one of the biggest decisions I was ever going to make. Call it what you like; a confirmation, a sign (Jdg.6:17), a test (Jdg.6:39) or whatever, what I was effectively doing was inviting God to intervene on my behalf and to be involved in the decision making process. I was asking Him to express His will and provide me with direction and leading to help me make one of the biggest decisions of my life (Gn.24:50-51). And that can't be a bad thing! Surely there is no one better to turn to than the omniscient, omnipotent, omnipresent heavenly Father!

So that's exactly what I did! I asked God to be involved and to participate in my situation, providing divine guidance. I believed God had led me to Violeta. Now it was time to ask for a specific response, for the divine confirmation I was after. I made the conditions of the response very clear. Abraham's servant asked for specific words to be spoken to him; Jonathan judged God's answer on what the Philistines actually said. I decided to write a letter to Violeta, expressing my feelings and interest in her, putting a time limit for a reply of two weeks. If I didn't hear from her within that time, I believed God's answer was "no."[16] I deliberately chose a period neither too long nor too short – Peru's postal system in those days was not the best! The time allotted also allowed for concentrated prayer and fasting, crying out to God for His answer, for His will.

The days passed. The two weeks were almost up. The last day arrived. I went to the post office to check our postal box – it was empty. I too felt empty, gutted. "Oh God, how could you do this? I

---

[16] For more specific conditions and an amazing outcome, cf. Ken Scott, 2020: *Life Stories of an Unworthy Servant,* p.14.

need her Lord. I need a helper to share my life with. But I believe in you and know you are sovereign. I love you and accept your will. I will honour your decision."

Later, back in the bungalow, Doreen Davies tapped on the window and called me over. There was a phone call for me. "Hello," I said, wondering who was phoning. "¡Hola! ¡Soy Violeta! ¡Estoy aquí en Cusco!" A stunned silence followed. Then the realisation! "Oh God, you are so good! She *has* contacted me, just within the timeframe! And even better, she is here in Cusco! Thank you!" The answer was "yes." God had given me His confirmation, His answer, His will, His guidance. *"Hallelu Yah!" "¡Gloria a Dios!"* Praise the Lord! I can't remember what language I used. Only that it was loud and that I was ecstatic!

What about Vio's side of the story? She too had been praying for a Christian partner (not a boyfriend), someone to share her life with and, together, to serve the Lord. Again, God's timing was immaculate, with everything falling into place. In response to my letter, she decided to travel to Cusco, staying with some friends. But there were a number of hurdles to be overcome first.

She was studying to become a school teacher and couldn't risk missing lectures. An activities week had been planned for the following week but, lo and behold, it was suddenly re-scheduled for a week earlier, meaning she could travel, without missing any classes! The icing on the cake was payment for her work at the local arts and craft shop (she had been waiting some time for the money)!

After a twelve hour overnight bus journey, she arrived in Cusco, had breakfast and went with her friend to the local University, not thinking to phone until the next day. At the University however, when her friend was busy, she noticed a phone booth and decided to call Nat and Doreen's house, just in the nick of time. If she'd waited any longer, it would have been too late! We arranged to meet up the next day and ended up chatting non-stop and having our first kiss! This was to be the start of an incredible journey which led to our engagement on Saturday 23rd December 1996, on a lovely hill top in San Jerónimo, Andahuaylas, with stunning views of the beautiful Chumbao valley. Needless to say there was a lot of excitement that weekend, culminating with a phone call to my folks and an official announcement in Violeta's local IEP church. As Vio was in her final year of studies before qualifying as a teacher and I was due for home leave assignment in March the following year, the wedding was set for the 21st February, 1997. We shall return to that wonderful day in more detail, in chapter 11.

I realise that the use of a confirmation or sign in this way will sit uncomfortably with some, and I respect and understand that entirely. I have tried to show examples from the Bible, and apply them to my own unique situation. It involved getting really, really close to God through prayer and fasting, which was certainly a good thing in itself. The answer might have been "yes," "no" or "not yet." I was totally willing to accept God's divine will, even if the answer was "no." I just wanted to hear from Violeta, expecting a reply by letter, which may sound simplistic. However, God could so easily have prevented us from meeting up; the letter could have been delivered too late, the activities week might not have been rescheduled, the phone call might have come a day later, or whatever. Again, make no mistake about it, I was totally willing to accept the answer, even if it was "no."[17]

---

[17] At Bible College I had been interested in another student. We hadn't started a relationship; I think we were both trying to determine the Lord's will and direction. So I implemented another guidance situation, setting aside a set time for prayer and fasting. On the very last evening, after returning from a prayer walk along the banks of the River Tweed, I didn't know what to

Thankfully, this was not the case. The living God had provided me with direction, leading me "on the right road." He had also provided me with my future wife. What could I do but bow down and worship my heavenly Father. (Gen.24:48).

---

do. There had been no answer. Darkness was falling as I rounded the corner to go up into the men's accommodation block. And there she was, standing just outside the door, despite the very strict separation policy adopted by the College. The girls never came over to the boy's area and vice versa. A smile spread across my face – "yes!" But she wasn't smiling. When we talked, she told me she had a boyfriend elsewhere. I went upstairs with mixed feelings; there was sadness to be sure. But there was also a warm glow in my heart. I felt God's presence so close. He had spoken to me. He had given me His answer, right at the end. It was no. He had someone else for me. I accepted the decision, got down on bended knee and gave thanks to the great living Lord.

"That's where my house used to be." The mud/boulder slide wreaked havoc in Santa Teresa (chp8).

"The Lost City of the Incas," Machu Picchu, in all its glory (chp 10).

Stuck in the mud! Travelling to Kcosñipata (chp 10).

Rock slide between Cusco and Andahuaylas. All the passengers had to
descend into the valley and then climb up the other side to connect with the
awaiting bus (chps. 8, 10).

TEE class in Huatta (chp. 10).

TEE graduates in Huanoquite (Moisés is 2 to the right of author (chp 10).

The author chatting to a fellow lecturer at the Chiguata Bible Institute (chp. 11).

The Big Day – the hotel porter delivered! (chp. 11).

CHAPTER 10
TEE and a Chance Encounter!

Cusco, the former Inca capital, stands at an altitude of 3399 metres (11,152 feet), some two and a half times the height of the UK's highest mountain, Ben Nevis.[18] It is a beautiful city, as anyone who has visited Machu Picchu can testify. The words of Psalm 125 seem to describe it so fittingly: *"As the mountains surround Jerusalem, so the LORD surrounds his people."* (If you've flown in by plane, you'll know all about it as the city is surrounded by mountains on three sides, making landing a little tricky)!

This was to be my new base, having completed language studies and cultural orientation in Arequipa. I was still single, living in an attractive bungalow at the back of the house rented by my Latin Link colleagues, Dr. Nat and Doreen Davies. They had taken me under their wings, helping me settle in quickly to my new abode. And of course those wonderful mountains brought great encouragement in themselves, reminding me that God was here with me, surrounding me with His presence, His protection and His love.

---

[18] When you arrive in Cusco, direct from sea level, be sure to lie down and rest for a short period, even if you're feeling great. At high altitude there is reduced air pressure and, with the thinner air, less oxygen available for the body. Hence each breath taken will contain fewer oxygen molecules, resulting in faster, rapid breathing. After acclimatisation the breathing rate does slow down, with the body making more red blood cells which help the oxygen to flow around the body. One of our wedding party in chapter 11 had a bad case of altitude sickness in Cusco.

I wasn't long in Cusco when my friend Favio, from Arequipa, paid a visit. We decided to hike the Inca trail and joined a group of nine tourists, a guide and various local porters. The full trail lasts for four days starting from kilometre 82, relatively close to Ollantaytambo, one of the main railway stations for Machu Picchu.[19] The Incas created thousands of kilometres of tracks and trails linking their important settlements. This one, although only 40 kilometres long (25 miles), takes you through some incredible scenery such as lush green cloud forest, panoramic views of the neighbouring valleys, steep mountain passes, Inca ruins en-route and the challenging accent on day two, up to dead Woman's Pass, at 4,200 metres (13,776 feet). Actually there were local kids on hand who, for a small fee, were willing to carry our rucksacks to the top! If the kids were a blessing in disguise, then the local porters were definitely our heroes! They were all Quechua folk from the Sacred Valley; tough, hardy men, each one carrying 25 kilograms on their backs, including the camping and cooking equipment, and food supplies. They would prepare breakfast, pack up camp, catch us up, then literally run past to go on ahead and have lunch ready further along the trail! With my few phrases of Quechua and the fact I had actually been to and knew people from one of their villages, I was able to connect and witness to them. The four days together provided plenty of opportunities to get to know each other as well; there were tourists from Chile, Argentina, Switzerland and England.

The trail ends at "perhaps the greatest end point of any multi-day hike on earth – the iconic Machu Picchu."[20] After an early start on the fourth day, we arrived before sunrise firstly at the entry check point, then at the Sun Gate (*Inti Punku*), with our first sighting of the

---

[19] A shorter two day trail is also available.
[20] www.alongdustyroads/incatrail 2019.

magnificent "Lost City of the Incas," one of the new "Seven Wonders of the World" and a UNESCO World Heritage listed site. At this point our guide really came to the fore, explaining in detail some of the incredible history and culture of the Incas. He showed us the central plaza flanked by the palace, the Sun Temple, other important buildings and the well organised irrigational system which provided adequate water for drinking, bathing and agriculture. The Inca engineers constructed a narrow conduit, which brought water into Machu Picchu, crossing a moat on a stone aqueduct, then flowing past the Sun Temple through a series of baths and fountains. The views were sensational, the city built on a narrow plateau sandwiched between two mountains, with near vertical drops on either side.

It is such a shame that the majority of tourists spend only a day at Machu Picchu, arriving by train in the morning, visiting the site, having lunch and then returning to Cusco in the late afternoon. Instead we decided to take our time, soaking up the ambience and feeling of peace the city radiates before descending by bus to *Aguas Calientes,* spending a night in a hostel. The town is renowned for the open air thermal baths, whose curative waters provided healing to our aching muscles! It was awesome to lie back in the steaming water, gazing up at the stars above! This was followed by a fabulous meal in one of the better restaurants in town and a cracking night's sleep!

With the short holiday over, it was time to get to work. Nat and I decided early on to jointly purchase a second hand 4 wheel drive vehicle, which would enable us to travel into the high Andes Mountains, where so many of our Quechua brothers and sisters lived. The vehicle, a Toyota land cruiser, with the insignia *"Servicio medico mobil"* was ideal.

I decided to revisit three congregations where Louis Sterkenburg had ministered, starting out with the church at Ranraq'asa. The road there was rocky, bumpy and gravelly but it was so worth it for the incredibly warm welcome we received from the *hermanos*. I say "we" because although I had started to learn Quechua and because many of the men and young people were all fluent in Spanish, there were occasions when it was essential to have an interpreter.[21] That interpreter was a man the Sterks had introduced me to, Moisés Luna Atayupanqui. (Nat and Doreen had encouraged me to take out a *pensión* with a local family, and just happened to arrange it with Moisés, his wife Amalia and their kids Daniel and Elisa)! Moisés travelled as not only translator, teacher and companion, but also as a friend and brother who taught me so much about the Quechua culture and customs. He shared about the similarities and resemblances between the old Inca religion and Christianity. Concepts of sin, confession, fasting, sacrifice and atonement, along with prayer, penance and purification, were important to the Incas. Their supreme deity was the creator, generally known as Viracocha who, according to Inca mythology, after travelling through the country instructing his people, set off across the Pacific from the shores of Ecuador, walking on the waves! Just as Inca farmers gave thanks to *Inti* and *Illapa,* so now the Quechua farmers give thanks to their Father in heaven. Just as fetishes were used to ward off evil spirits, so now prayer is used calling upon the blood of the Saviour for protection and blessing. Just as coincidences were never regarded as purely chance, so now is there an awareness of the living God who is involved and in control of each person's life. Just as great faith was placed in the Inca priests for healing, so today there is a need for a similar display of faith. And just as then there was a communal spirit of helpfulness and sufficiency, so the Church today is seen to be a source, or at least a means of providing, that same degree of

---

[21] I made a start at learning Quechua, studying for seven weeks at the Andina Post Graduate College, before the work load got too much.

helpfulness and sufficiency. We had many wonderful conversations on our long journeys and remain great friends to this day.

The natural step was to restart the TEE classes in Ranraq'asa which we did. It didn't take long for word to get around and within a short period of time the two other churches came on board, in Huatta and Huanoquite. Then God provided that moment of divine guidance once again, totally out of the blue, with a knock on the door! The Director of the Cusco Synod's Theological Commission of the IEP paid a visit. The Synod had just met and decided, without consultation of any kind, to appoint me as Director of the TEE programme. In one minute my responsibility for three groups now had the potential of escalating to over 250! Without even asking if I was interested! Such is Peru where just about anything can happen! However, as the timing was spot on, as I was young, bold and eager and, above all, believed this to be God's will and guidance, I acknowledged the incredible honour given me and gladly accepted the massive challenge.

The Cusco Synod, made up of fifteen Presbyteries, covers a vast area stretching from the high Andes in the south (Espinar, Alto Canas), down to the Amazon jungle in the east (Alto Urubamba, Yanatile). Moisés and I were soon off on our travels on a regular basis.

TEE is a fabulous method of teaching theology in the *Sierra*. Many of the *hermanos* are farmers, hence going away to study full time at Bible College was an unrealistic option. Instead, the programme effectively takes the college to them, as they study the material at home, meeting in groups with their tutor in the local church on a fortnightly basis. After four or five months, when the book was completed, Moisés and I would arrive for a *taller,* a workshop, in which we picked out and developed various themes from the finished manual. This would culminate with an exam and the purchase of the next study book for those wishing to continue.

Each Presbytery could approach me if they were interested in starting the programme; some were keen and enthusiastic, others less so. As they were often located geographically close to each other, we could hold a workshop in Yauri for example, then move on to Alto Canas and finally Espinar, three days to cover three Presbyteries. It was great when my father in law, Alejandro, was able to accompany me on one such three day trip. Even he was amazed when we were each presented with a massive block of cheese for breakfast in Alto Canas! This was one of the ways the *hermanos* were able to express their thanks. We always seemed to end up with bigger portions than everyone else! On other shorter trips my brother in law Herzon, also came along. He was able to take part in the workshops and would later spend two years on Logos 2 with Operation Mobilisation. Both he and his family are very active in their local church in Andahuaylas.

Other Presbyteries and Consistories were more isolated and difficult to get to. An extract from my June 1998 prayer letter gives you an idea:

A trip to Kcosñipata

Early Wednesday 15 April, Mark set off to visit our most distant Consistory, Kcosñipata, accompanied by a Peruvian Pastor and Amalia de Luna (who cooked all my delicious meals)! Each one of us had a different reason for going; Mark to form a new TEE group in the area, Isaías, the Pastor, to speak at a convention and officiate at a wedding and Amalia, also travelling for the wedding as "madrina," or lady of honour/Godmother to the bride.

People had warned us about the state of the road. Trucks travelled "in" on a Monday, Wednesday and Friday, returning to Cusco on Tuesday, Thursday and Saturday. Everything was fine until we reached a village called Chuntachaca. Our way forward was blocked by a truck stuck solidly in the mud. Three hours later, after unloading all its cargo, it finally squelched out of the hole. Half an hour later it was our turn to be stuck in the same spot, despite the power of the 4 wheel drive Toyota land cruiser. Thankfully a lorry behind was able to toe us out and, at the second attempt, with the car empty bar driver, the "bridge" was crossed. The horrendous road conditions continued for a further ten kilometres until we pulled up exhausted, but thankful to be here, in the town of Patria, a fourteen hour journey.

But it was really worth it. Three days later two of us returned to Cusco, leaving behind five new TEE groups with a total of 38 students. The "hermanos" were so pleased to see us and a good number of Bibles, books etc. were sold. Mark is due to return, DV, in September."

But if it was difficult for us, think of what some of our students had to endure. On one trip to Sausaya, the river was totally impassable. We had to meet in another town instead, the students wading across two rivers, chest deep, to get to the workshop. 40 made it! Two brothers travelled a day and a night to get to Urcos in time for the TEE class. In Huatta, with each church taking it in turn to host the class, providing a meal afterwards, some of the *hermanos* had to walk 2-3 hours, often arriving for the class with sweat dripping off their faces, due to the difficult mountainous terrain. Others travelled by bicycle, on horseback, on foot or by grabbing a lift from a passing goods lorry, often in the bitter, freezing cold (we woke up to snow in Yauri). Their hunger and commitment to study God's word was astonishing. Many of the students came from poor, remote farming communities. For many, leaving the farms behind and going to study at Bible College was not an option. Money was tight, but did not deter or dampen their interest and desire.

We were very encouraged when, on the 16th May, 1999, 14 students from Huatta, near Cusco, finished the course. Many of them occupied positions of leadership in the different churches they represented and were instrumental in pastoring their flocks and evangelising the local communities. Moisés and I brought along a few treats; 2 litre bottles of Coca Cola bought in bulk, cakes and biscuits for desert. The *hermanas* served up a delicious soup containing potatoes, barley, vegetables and small pieces of meat, followed by *cuy* (guinea pig) with more potatoes, a vegetable salad and *yatán,* a delicious sauce made from herbs, chillies, cheese, garlic, olive oil, a little water and seasoning.[22] What a feast! The fellowship was incredible; chatting and joking, hearing all sorts of stories from both past and present. Just as we were getting up to go, *hermano Juan Cruz,* that year's elected church President, took us by surprise. He wanted to know if the group could go on, continuing to study at Diploma level. The books were not subsidised, coming from the SIM office in Lima. What could we do? I explained the costs involved and the time it would take to complete this new level. I then asked how many wanted to go on. Tears filled my eyes when I saw their reply; every single one had put their hand up! Praise God! He is so good! His people are so wonderful!

The appointment as Director left me totally in charge, with a free hand to design the TEE programme as desired. I decided to appoint Co-ordinators for each Presbytery, whose responsibility was to visit

---

[22] There are over 3000 varieties of potatoes in Peru, differing in size, shape and colour! The Quechua speakers were the first people in the world to cultivate potatoes, sometimes cutting terraces into the slopes of the mountain sides to provide agricultural land. Shortly after 1536, the Spanish brought the potato to Europe. In 1586 Sir Thomas Harriot introduced them to mainland Britain. They arrived in Ireland in 1589, thanks to Sir Walter Raleigh.

each group at least once during the four to five months, making sure everything was running smoothly and ironing out any problems. They were nominated by their Presbyteries and would use the visits to pastor and minister to not only the TEE students, but also to the churches as a whole. These gifted leaders contributed enormously to the success of the programme, people like Pascual Maggue in Layo, Epifanio Conza in Yauri, Benito Chino in Alto Canas and Amando Accostupa in Anta.

Nat, Doreen and I were all invited to teach, at different times, in the Sicuani Bible Institute (SBI), the theological centre for the Cusco Synod. It wasn't long before the Director, Noé Huahuachampi, invited Nat and I onto the board, along with an incredible servant called Hilda Valeriano and one other *hermano*. This typifies Latin Link's policy of working alongside the local church, providing help, assistance and encouragement wherever possible. I made a point of bringing the TEE programme under the auspices of the SBI, offering our graduates the chance to have the graduation ceremony held in their local churches, or in Sicuani, together with the full time students.

The board had to meet regularly in order to prepare for a very important upcoming event; the SBI's 50th anniversary. Here's how my prayer letter read:

Enter his gates with thanksgiving and his courts with praise; give thanks to him and praise his name. For the LORD is good and his love endures for ever; his faithfulness continues through all generations (Psm.100:4-5).

"Sicuani's 50th anniversary was a great success!" That seemed to be the general impression after a very busy week of activities. The programme commenced with a three day conference with

workshops and expositions. This was followed by various talks by two *hermanos* from Lima and one from England, Donald Ford. It was such an encouragement that both Donald and Marge (past teachers) could be present, along with Hilda Brisco (who speaks fluent Quechua). A number of the Institute's pioneer students also attended and were presented with a special book to mark the occasion.

The conference was replaced by a Synod convention with numbers continuing to rise (by Sunday we estimated that approximately 1000 people were present). The *día central* included a graduation service (with, among others, six TEE students from Alto Canas) and, one of the highlights for me, a recorded message from Leslie Hoggarth, heavily involved in the Institute's foundation. The Psalmist's words about God's faithfulness continuing through all generations, was very evident in Sicuani. We have much indeed to "shout for joy to the LORD!"

I was so proud of my TEE graduates. They excelled firstly in the football tournament, playing against a local professional team adorned in crisp, clean, sponsored, shirts with names and numbers. My team (I was the coach after all!) wore an eclectic assortment of kit, a smorgasbord of sorts! We drew 1-1, going out on penalties. Then my heart just about burst as they participated in the evening's "specials," the five men dressed in their beautiful, hand-woven, multicoloured, intricately designed ponchos and woollen waist coats; the one *hermana* equally splendid in her embroidered skirt and shawl. They sang their hearts out, accompanied by their own guitars and mandolins and fully deserved the rapturous round of applause that followed, accompanied by shouts of *"¡Otro! ¡Otro!"*.

The TEE programme continued to flourish and the SBI found herself with not only around 30 internal students each semester, but 350 external ones as well.[23] I also found myself with help from another great, long serving, missionary colleague, Maaike Hopma from Holland. She had worked in different parts of Peru including Urcos, Quillabamba, Pisco (south of Lima), and now Cusco. She blended in immediately, taking over a number of groups and helping enormously with the administration.

Meanwhile the invitations to teach in Bible Colleges kept coming. I made various trips back to Ayaviri, Talavera and Sicuani and later taught in both the IEP's and the Assembles of God's night Bible Colleges in Cusco. One of the local Pastors, Bernardo Justiniani, turned out to be a tremendous blessing. As well as pastoring the Santiago church in Cusco, he worked for a Christian radio station which broadcast primarily in Quechua. During one of my courses, Advanced Homiletics, I was able to record the student's "Thought for the Day," which Bernardo was later able to use on his programme. I don't brandish the term "man of God" around too often, but would not have the slightest hesitation in using it to describe this great servant who is now in the presence of his beloved Saviour.

There were also invitations to teach in the smaller Bible Colleges in the jungle, at La Quebrada and Kiteni. The latter sticks out for a number of reasons. Again, my prayer letter explains why:

I set off on a two day trek to Kiteni, firstly by train to Quillabamba and then seven hours further in to the jungle on a dirt road. Kiteni acts as a base for the IEP and boasts a large church cum evangelical school and a small Bible Institute. I arrived here sweating profusely, to teach two courses in the Institute (Homiletics and the Pentateuch). The two weeks proved to be very memorable indeed:

---

[23] The TEE programme was eventually handed over to Pastor Leopoldo Aguilar. The number of students soon increased to over 389!

+ In the evenings the place seemed to come alive with many insects having a taste for some nice sweet gringo blood! Thankfully a nearby stream provided refreshment for the body.

+It was here where I tasted more delicious coffee. Other local products included bananas, cocoa, beans, yuca and various different fruits such as papaya, avocados, mandarins and oranges. We ate bananas in various different forms; skinned, fried and boiled! We also had beans, beans and more beans, which led to a few embarrassing moments in the classes! One hermano also brought in an interesting animal called a "picura", an anteater look alike, that tasted delicious (cross between chicken and rabbit).

But it was great to be here to help and encourage the students in their studies. Many of them would go on to be the future leaders in the churches and communities they represented. The mornings were set aside for 2 x 1½ hour classes, which sometimes continued into the afternoon. However, there were also two afternoons of sport and one of practical work such as helping to make the "adobe" mud bricks used for constructing houses and buildings. I always enjoyed exploring the local area and, during an afternoon off, hiked up to explore the "disused" landing strip. I also enjoyed playing footie with the students and local children. Well there I was playing in goals when lo and behold a BBC film crew arrived, setting up camp on the side of our pitch! They were en-route to the famous "Pongos de Mainique" – the dreaded white water rapids further on from Kiteni. And who should step off the bus but Michael Palin. "What are you doing here," he asked? "You took the words right out of my mouth," I replied! He was in Peru recording the documentary series "Full Circle."

We had a great chat; he really is a lovely man. I didn't make it into his TV documentary but he does mention Kiteni in his book:

If Quillabamba was the end of the railway then Kiteni, which we reach in late afternoon, is the end of the road. There is a short trail beyond, but to all intents and purposes there is no way north from here except by river.

We rumble down the main street, which can only claim to be a street because it has buildings on both sides...We ask where we can camp for the night and are directed through the village to a hard grass football pitch. Local children are in the middle of a game...As Barry and his team set up camp... the children watch our every move as if we are men from Mars. We eat around a table in an open-sided mosquito-netted mess tent. [24]

He also mentions meeting a theology teacher from Armagh, Northern Ireland. Guess that must be me!

Around about the same time, I was elected on to the Peru Executive, with Nat in charge. How these folk manage to handle the work load I'll never know, people like Nat and previous team leaders Dr Simon Baker and Marcelo Durst. Business meetings were held every three months, mostly in Lima but occasionally in Cusco. It was a joy to catch up with the Jameson family again, who were now based in Lima. John was preaching at his local church and so I went along to see how he got on. Man did he do well! As homiletics was one of my speciality subjects, he asked me how it went. I couldn't fault him on anything. It was totally gripping. In fact I did mention that if he had made an appeal for people to come forward (popular in some Peruvian churches), there would have been quite a response!

I do need to mention Violeta at this juncture. She would go on to prove such a valuable asset to the work, partly due to the fact that she spoke Quechua but also because of her qualifications as a

---

[24] Michael Palin, 1998, *Full Circle,* pages 258-259.

teacher. She obtained a Degree in teaching from Cusco's main University, *San Antonio Abad*. As well as working in a primary school close to Cusco, she was also able to help in the SBI teaching Advanced Spanish and Arts and Crafts. Vio in the past had worked in her Uncle's business during the holidays in Lima, hand painting items to sell in the local tourist markets. We have many examples in the house which exemplify her talents! Anyway, the handicraft classes were a great success. Vio bought 14 clay pots in the Cusco market – one for each student. She then taught them how to cover the pots with a chalk substance before going on to apply the paint. The end result was a beautifully hand painted floral vase or pot (not in every case!) which could be taken home by the students, a real novelty indeed. The Diploma students were a little put out as numbers had to be limited for the class, although they were promised first choice next time!

She was also involved in the local TEE work, taking the roll, correcting homework, teaching new choruses, selling hymn books and Bibles. It was such a joy to be able to work together for the Lord.

But again, I'm getting ahead of myself. It's time to go back to a very, very special day for us both – the 21st February, 1997.

CHAPTER 11
The Big Day – and Beyond!

Back in 1997, the best way to get to Peru from Scotland was to fly Glasgow to Amsterdam, Amsterdam to Aruba/Bonaire, then, after a 1½ hour break for the crew change over, on to Lima. It was a long, long journey for Mum, Dad, brother Jamie, sister Zelda, best man John Haley and two members from my home church's missionary board, Ronnie Cartwright and John Hunter.

John Haley, of course, had been my best mate at Bible College, the guy from Southbank Mission. In many ways this was a first for John – first passport, first time out of the UK, first time on a plane and first time singing a solo in Spanish! He did so well, his beautiful bass voice belting out the words to Carl Boberg/Stuart Hine's "How Great Thou Art," one of our favourites. I was so honoured when, later on, John married Debbie and asked me to be his best man.

We met up on their arrival, spending a couple of interesting days in the capital. At one time American Airlines scheduled flights from New York, Dallas and Miami direct to Cusco, thus avoiding Lima. However, Lima has developed considerably over the years and, in parts, is a very beautiful city indeed. It is actually the gastronomic capital of the Americas, having no less than a third of the top 15 best Latin American restaurants in the world. Dishes such as *lomo saltado* (marinated stir fried steak, rice, homemade chips, onions, tomatoes, chilli, seasoning and parsley to add when serving) and *caldo de gallina,* (a delicious soup consisting of broth, hen, potatoes, chillies a boiled egg and noodles), are an absolute delight.[25] The more adventuresome of the party, (namely myself), enjoyed one of Peru's most famous plates; *ceviche.* the fresh raw fish, direct from the Pacific Ocean, is cooked or marinated in lemon, lime and other citric juices, accompanied with *cancha* (Peruvian roasted corn), sweet potato, red onion, chilli, garlic, coriander, seasoning and a lettuce garnish. You can tell my wife is a great cook! Nowadays there are Peruvian restaurants in most of the world's capitals (in London for example). Treat yourself sometime (and try *chicha morada,* a delicious non-alcoholic purple coloured fruit drink!).

The highlight in Lima was definitely a visit to one of the beautiful parks, *Parque del Amor,* in Miraflores. John Hunter was in charge of organising a small *ceilidh,*[26] the traditional Scottish folk music and dance popular at weddings and other social gatherings. He had called for a practise in the very aptly named park! The music blared out from the portable mini speakers. We took our partners and did our best to dance to *The Dashing White Sergeant* and the *Gay Gordons.* Being fully engrossed in the dancing, we didn't notice a crowd gathering. As the music came to an end, loud clapping and cheering rang out from the local Limeños, who were greatly amused and delighted at their first glimpse of Scottish dancing!

It was time to take a rather interesting flight on to Andahuaylas, in an old, Russian propeller, cargo plane, with no windows or seats! We were accompanied on the journey by various Peruvians, animals and massive cargo bags. The air hostess used a megaphone to give out the

---

[25] The thicker broths are also delicious, containing meat, potatoes, yucca, sweet potato, corn, leeks, turnip, cabbage, parsnips and a fabulous broth; a meal in itself! The trick is to dunk a small slice of chilli into the soup, then removing it before the broth becomes too overpowering! Be sure to squeeze in some juice from those incredible, small, round lemons. *Chupe de Camarones,* using river prawns, is another delight. You'll notice that chilli makes a regular appearance in Peruvian cooking; in the past I rarely ate any dish with chilli or rice. Things were to change for the better on arriving in Peru!

[26] A Gaelic word meaning *"gathering"* or *"party."*

safety instructions and eventually passed round little bottles of the famous yellow coloured Inca cola. Amazingly Zelda, who hadn't slept a wink on the flights from Glasgow, was sound asleep within minutes!

On arrival, our entourage was escorted to the hotel in Andahuaylas. As there was a problem with the return flight, Cherry and I had to dash off to obtain tickets for a different plane, which was departing a day earlier than scheduled. Meanwhile Mum and Dad stuffed a wad of notes into the hotel porter's hand and, by pointing to a floral arrangement, tried to convey the message that we needed the same for the wedding. Preparations continued for the "Big Day;" and what a day it was! The church looked magnificent, the inside decked out with flowers and banners, the words from Ecclesiastes 4:12 taking pride of place behind the pulpit.[27] Peruvians are so artistic and practical when it comes to decorating churches, halls etc. Colourful flower petals, in the form of hearts, were laid in each aisle, one with the letter V, the other with an M. On the outside of the building, miniature Peruvian and British flags flew in harmony, side by side.

If the church looked magnificent, the bride went one better! Violeta looked stunning in her wedding dress and tiara! Mark managed into a suit for the first time in 3½ years! The service flowed beautifully in Spanish, English and Quechua. We were so pleased to see so many folk present, especially the seven who had travelled all the way from the UK. Our colleague and friend Alex Donnelly officiated and performed the wedding ceremony. Pastor Isaías Calle preached in both Spanish and English, referring to Peru's famous 3-1 victory over Scotland in the 1978 World Cup! He went on to add that we were now both on the same team! Cherry Noble led the service, with a number of other people taking part, including Ronnie Cartwright. It really struck home when he stood up to say that both he and John

---

[27] *A cord of three strands is not quickly broken* (Ecc.4:12).

Hunter were here representing the congregation of Ayr Baptist Church. What a church! What support and dedication to their missionaries, flying all this way! For us this really was another example of Christianity in its purest form; people willing to leave jobs and family behind, in order to show their backing and support to the fullest. Thanks so much guys!

Other Latin Link personnel, including John Chapman, also attended. With all the Alarcón Altamirano relatives in attendance, including Violeta's sister Begoña and her husband Robert from Oklahoma, brother Harry from Lima plus friends and the *hermanos* from the church, every seat was taken. People even stood outside, looking in from the open windows. When the joyous couple left the building, massive, beautiful bouquets of flowers were placed into our hands. The porter from the hotel had delivered!

The reception turned out to be a mixture of things both Peruvian and British. The hall was immaculately adorned, the food exquisite, the speeches both touching and funny. And yes, the *ceilidh* was a huge success! It was followed by some of the beautiful, slower dances from the Andahuaylas region.

Mr and Mrs Walker junior later flew back to Lima where our little party spent a fabulous day on the beach at Pucusana. This delightful little seaside village not far from the capital, with a beautiful harbour, sandy beach and paddle boats (today there are even jet skies!), was the idealistic setting for a delicious meal of fresh seafood and *ceviche* direct from the Pacific Ocean. Mum tried her best to persuade John Haley to use plenty of sun tan lotion. Sadly, he didn't heed her advice, and spent a rather uncomfortable flight back to the UK!

This was to be the start of a lot of travelling for the newlyweds, firstly to the Latin Link team conference in Kawai, where our colleagues who couldn't make it to the wedding, were able to meet Violeta for the first time. The conference was followed by a brief honeymoon en route to London for the start of our first home-leave assignment.

HOME LEAVE ASSIGNMENT

Mum and Dad, along with Pastor Noel McCullins, organised a special service/welcome home celebration in Ayr Baptist Church on Saturday 22nd March, 1997. Noel led the service of blessing, after which a piper was on hand (thanks Gavin), to welcome everyone into the beautifully adorned lower hall, where a delicious meal was served for over 120 people. The Rev. Douglas Paterson, a lecturer from NBC and former missionary in Rwanda, gave thanks. The meal was followed by various speeches of thanks, a 25 minute video of the wedding, a Peruvian quiz, a delicious cake and an excellent rendering of a Robbie Burns poem by my niece. Thanks Katy!

It was such a joy to see so many of our family and friends present, many of whom had supported us so faithfully over the years both prayerfully and financially. Their contribution to the success of our ministry cannot be overstated. We simply could not have made it without their support and love. The best way I can try to show the incredible role they played is to use a true story shared to the church in 2008 by our elder and head of the Missionary Board, George Campbell. He referred to a bed-ridden old lady from Inverness who had supported him in prayer over the years. When George visited Agnes he found picture after picture of missionaries and world leaders up on the walls. "Where's mine," he asked? "Over there

George. I pray for you every day. In fact, I remember the exact time I pray for you – 10 o'clock in the morning."

George pulled out his watch and showed it to her. It had stopped at exactly 10 o'clock. The reason for that was due to a car accident, quite a bad one, yet amazingly the only thing broken was the watch. "Thank you so much Agnes for praying for me," George said. Her persistent praying had worked!

Later, when George met with the ruler of Zambia in the President's office, he noticed a picture of Agnes. When she passed on to be with the Lord, a deputation of 14 children travelled over from Africa to be at her funeral. What a prayer warrior!

We had plenty of Agnes's as well, both individuals and prayer groups! Travelling in the high Andes was extremely dangerous to say the least. Drivers were known to fall asleep at the wheel, the buses careening down into the vast ravines (I often travelled overnight by this method). Enormous trucks sped along the narrow mountain roads transporting their products from one place to another. Yet we never seemed to encounter them at the dangerously tight hair pin bends. I can only remember having one puncture in all my travels, occurring just as we were entering the town of Yauri. If it had happened way up in the remote mountains, it would have delayed us considerably. And of course over the years our prayer letters were faithfully sent out by people like Pam Craig, John Hunter, George and Fay Campbell, Isabel Paterson and others involved in designing (Alan Harkness), typing and printing (Agnes, Phyllis and Edith; all employed by the Martin family, to mention just a few). Sorry if I've missed anyone! Thank you all so much for the incredibly important part you all played.

During our home leave assignment we visited churches, schools, prayer groups, conferences (LL Scotland and Northern Ireland), NBC and two prisons (with South American prisoners) throughout the UK and in Holland (when we were wonderfully looked after by the Sterkenburgs). It was a privilege to be able to share our work and vision, meeting so many wonderful people in so many different places.

Vio was amazing despite having to move around so much during our first months of marriage, and dealing with mental tiredness from learning a new language – been there! Here are some of the many questions people asked her on our travels:

"Do you like our country?" "Is it a little cold for you here?" "Do you miss your Mum and Dad?" "What about the food?" To which she replied:

"I really have enjoyed the time here immensely, seen many interesting things and met some truly wonderful people. The biggest frustration for me is not being able to say all I want to in English but this is improving all the time. Yes, I really like Scotland, Ireland, England, Wales and Holland. In some parts it was quite cold but the weather has been pretty good so far. I miss Mum and Dad a great deal but phone them every fortnight. My favourite meal is, wait for it, fish and chips!"

Talking of fish and chips, it was lovely to catch up with Leslie Hoggarth in St. Andrews. We found Leslie glued to the TV watching the end of the England v Ireland rugby match. "Would you mind holding on to the end of the match," he asked? "Not at all Leslie, not at all!" After a cup of tea and some chat with Violeta in Spanish and Quechua, it was off for a walk along one of those beautiful beaches before buying delicious fish suppers from his favourite chippie and heading back to the house.

Perhaps the largest group in our church was the Women's Fellowship, which Vio always attended and thoroughly enjoyed. It offers tremendous companionship, support, encouragement, fellowship and fun and was ably run by people like Betty Barrie, Anne Martin, Mary Clark, June Dornan, Marion Cartwright and many others. We put on a special Peruvian evening with slides, info, a short meditation and a cooking display by Violeta (including *ceviche*)!

We are indebted to Delia and Rob Hyder who fed and lodged us so well, during our month in Edinburgh. Violeta was able to advance her English at the Basil Paterson Language Foundation. Their love and support remain with us to this day.

RETURNING TO CUSCO

Sunday 31st August, 1997 is a date we will never forget. We were flying out from Heathrow, en route to Lima via the US. Security was tight; even the suitcases had to be opened and checked. Sadly, one of our lovely souvenirs from Holland fell out and smashed to pieces. That was nothing to the news that followed. Princess Diana was dead. The news was a total shock to the world.

Our work with the TEE programme and in the various Bible Institutes has been mentioned already. Violeta had to give up her teaching job etc. due to a very special occasion. This is what she wrote in our April 2000 prayer letter:

I was kept busy last year studying for my degree in Education at the Cusco University. God's timing was wonderful and I was able to finish the course just before Christmas, allowing me to concentrate on another extremely important matter! Daniel Greg was born on Friday 4th February at 8.11 pm. Everybody was amazed at his size! We praise the Lord for the safe birth. Little Greg sends his love and greetings!

The whole family was overjoyed, with visits from both Andahuaylas and Armagh! It was so good to enjoy quality family time together which culminated with a short holiday in Paracas, a beautiful coastal town 152 miles south of Lima. The highlight was definitely a boat trip to the uninhabited Ballestas Islands, home to a large range of bird and sea life, including sea lions, pelicans and penguins. The trip back to harbour offered fabulous views of the peninsula's famous candelabra shaped geoglyph, etched into the hillside during prehistoric times.

The words of Gloria and William Gaither's hymn *Because He lives* could not be more appropriate:

How sweet to hold a new-born baby, and feel the pride and joy he gives;

But greater still the calm assurance, this child can face uncertain days because He lives.

SECOND HOME LEAVE ASSIGNMENT

We arrived back in the UK on March 15th 2001, spending the weekend in Sheffield with Zelda, before getting into Ayr on the Monday. The welcome we received was amazing; it was great to catch up with folk again after 3½ years.

On Sunday 25th, in our home church, Greg was dedicated to the Lord; Gavin Smith (the Scottish LL coordinator) preaching. It was a lovely service, with nearly all the family present. We had much to praise the Lord for.

Ronnie Cartwright was instrumental in the planning of the various meetings which ranged from church services, visits to prayer meetings, conferences, a LL Action Group, Sunday schools, youth fellowships, Scripture Union groups, Women's meetings, an old folk's home and a Senior's club. The visit to the latter was memorable, held in the Alloway village community hall, just opposite Robbie Burn's cottage, in Ayr. As the slides presentation progressed, with the backing music of the *Condor Pasa* blasting out loudly, the floor began to vibrate and move with all the foot tapping!

The visits were organised in blocks, such as a visit to the Edinburgh area, Newcastle/Sheffield/Atherton, Northern Ireland, Oxford/London/Welling/Farnham, Wooler/Middlesbrough, Chirnside/Musselburgh/Jedburgh/Lythham St. Annes and the Aberdeen area. It was so encouraging to hear of one man called to Bible College following one of our meetings in Edinburgh!

It was so nice to see so many of our faithful supporters once again and to enjoy their superb hospitality. The trend at the time was to have two desserts for pudding. Violeta was able to politely decline the kind offer to sample the two. It would have been insensitive of Mark to have done likewise!

BACK TO AREQUIPA

We returned to Peru in June 2003 and, after a short time with family in Lima, travelled on to our new base, Arequipa. However, on arrival, there was a problem with the promised accommodation. The house we were due to move into had been rented to a missionary who was back in the UK and who might not be returning. The lease had expired but her possessions (including the dog) were still there, a Peruvian family occupying the house for security reasons. Meanwhile we stayed in the LL visitor's flat waiting. While the flat was adequate, though a little basic, it was impossible to unpack fully, to set up home and to install an internet system (Greg was 3 at the time as well). The waiting went on and on. A month passed. We kept asking about the house and decided to "go the extra mile," hoping and praying for guidance. After two months we could take no more; it looked like this could go on forever. On the morning we were scheduled to meet to talk about the accommodation, God guided us through the following verse:

When Peter came to Antioch, I opposed him to his face (Gal 2:15).

The context, of course, relates to Peter drawing back and separating himself from the Gentiles (verses 12-21). However, we felt very clearly that God was speaking to us through this Scripture, providing guidance in our own dilemma, telling us that enough was enough. It was time to speak up. We did just that on a Friday morning. On the following Monday, a man knocked on our door (his parents worked for the same mission as the lady on extended home leave), saying he was intent on emptying the house and handing over the keys later that evening. He was as good as his word and by 7 pm the house was ours. It was that simple, but it took God to push us a little to solve the problem! Once again, He had spoken and provided guidance through His "*living and active*" word.

It was a joy to move in to our new abode. We were kept busy, getting the house painted (well done Vio), furniture moved in etc. It was an ideal location, not far from the city centre, close to the *Colegio Internacional,* and with a market around the corner selling fresh meat, fruit and vegetables. There was even a guy every day selling fresh, unpasteurised milk.

It was also a joy to get stuck in to the work. My main ministry was teaching, still in Sicuani at the SBI, but also more locally at the IEP Chiguata Bible Institute, close to Arequipa. It was another one of those fabulous working relationships between the Director, Pastor Santos Valero, other Peruvian Pastors and personnel and missionaries from both Latin Link and SIM. Both Alan Turner and his colleague Mike Thompson from Sheffield had been heavily involved, organising a Step team at some stage. As usual the work was very intensive, classes beginning at 7.30 in the morning and finishing around lunch time, with only a half hour break in between. Hence the early morning bus on most occasions, the exception being when Jeff or Eric, our SIM neighbours, were involved in the teaching as well.

During the previous home leave assignment, I submitted a 40,000 word thesis entitled; *Hope and Encouragement for the Oppressed; the Perspective of the Apocalypse of John on the Crises facing its First Readers.* Quite a mouthful, but it did tie in with my work with the Quechua *hermanos,* many of whom find great solace and encouragement from the book of Revelation. The last book in the Bible belongs to the genre of ancient Jewish and Christian literature known as apocalypses, or apocalyptic literature. Many of the characteristic traits of apocalyptic literature are to be found in Revelation, traits such as visual imagery and symbolism, the judgment of the wicked and the vindication of the saints, the eschatological element and the interest in otherworldly beings and places. These apocalypses function, at least in part, to offer hope and comfort to a group in crisis.[28] Despite the difficulties that people sometimes experienced, encouragement came from the knowledge that God was in fact in control. People were encouraged to view current events in a new light, seeing beyond the present to a time in the future when He would bring order out of the chaos. God would, at the appropriate time, bring history to a climax. Injustice and oppression would be swept away. Things would get better. God would be victorious and that victory would extend to his people as well. Apocalyptic literature then, offered hope and encouragement by creating an alternative vision, an alternative concept of reality.

In the book of Revelation, the frightening, disintegrative effects of evil (persecution, death, suffering, discrimination, injustice, poverty etc.) are reversed by the imaginative reconstruction of another world and another reality where things are different. [29] That other world and other reality are referred to by John on numerous occasions when dealing with the theme of eternal life. Eternal life offers the Christian immortality in the presence of God. Eternal life signifies the complete absence of physical and spiritual want, offering instead a life full of abundance and perfection that will last forever. It means belongingness to God, which implies divine ownership and divine citizenship. Thus God is not distant and aloof; instead He is immediate, His very dwelling among His people. Those who are His

---

[28] So Hanson, 1976, *Apocalypse, Genre in The Interpreter's Dictionary of the Bible*, supplementary volume, p.27. He adds that Rev 1:19 indicates that the primary function of the book is to "disclose to the elect the secret of *what is and what is to take place*, thereby serving to comfort the oppressed and encourage them to remain faithful to their beliefs." Rowland states that Revelation's purpose "is to reveal something hidden which will enable the readers to view their present situation from a completely different perspective...The apocalypses offered a basis for hope in a world where God seemed to be restrained" (Rowland C., 1990, *The Apocalypse: Hope, Resistance and the Revelation of Reality, in Ex Auditu* 6 pp. 136-37).
[29] "The greater the capacity to imagine future pleasures...the greater the weight these will carry in current choices...future scenarios and image need to be frequently refreshed" (So Smith I, 2002, *A Rational Choice Model of the Book of Revelation, in Journal for the Study of the New Testament* 85, p.113).

will enjoy the unmediated presence of God for ever and ever.[30] It is a theme of great joy and happiness. No longer will there be death or mourning or crying or pain. The old age will pass away, the new one begin. These were the feelings of expectation and desire that John longed for the Christian to have – words that looked beyond the reality of daily life, taking the reader into a deeper spiritual realm where the oppressors are no longer in control. John's response to the difficult times he writes about is to offer hope from the past (Christ's death bringing freedom from bondage and misery), relating it to the present and prophesying about the future when the New Jerusalem will be established in all its glory. These are the words and beliefs that his readers must cling on to.

Hence the attraction to the book of Revelation for many of the Quechua *hermanos*. Despite the poverty, discrimination, difficulties and disappointments that many of them face, their Christian faith remains strong. They seem able to almost ignore the physical hardships and pains that life brings, instead concentrating on the spiritual side of life and on their relationship with God. Their hope is grounded in the fact that although many of them are physically poor, they are actually spiritually rich. In the eyes of society they may sometimes seem to be insignificant and unimportant; in the eyes of God however, they are very special people indeed. They are citizens of God's kingdom. They are His children. They are His people. Thus the Quechua Christians seem able to view their current circumstances in a new light by firstly believing that, in the present, a special relationship exists between them and God and, secondly, that in the future things will change.[31] Suffering and oppression will not always be present.[32] Better times lie ahead.[33]

---

[30] So Rowland, Ibid, p.142.
[31] This viewpoint is not unique to the Quechua Christians. Martin Haworth, a former missionary in the Philippines, relates how *the tribal people…counted it as such a joy to be in*

Perhaps what Susan Sontag advises, with referral to literature in general, has relevance to readers of the book of Revelation: "What is important now is to recover our senses. We must learn to see more, hear more, feel more."[34] Peterson states that men and women "have not gotten new ideas out of the Apocalypse – they have found new feelings."[35]

Hence their interest in this fabulous book in the New Testament, one that is not read as much as it should be, often relegated merely to a curiosity in the Bible.[36] And hence Santos's request for the Book to be one of the courses I had to teach. But before that I had to return to the UK to defend my work at a viva examination in Aberdeen University, held on the 6th November, 2003. Present at the viva was one of the New Testament lecturers from the University, Dr Simon

---

*Christ. Christ was their everything, their "very great reward." They quite literally longed to be with Him in a heaven where the huge injustices they faced day by day would no longer happen. This helped them endure their daily lot, such as keeping their hope in Christ in their great poverty; coping prayerfully with illness with little or no resource to medicine or health care, and the injustices caused by aggressive outsiders snatching their land or carrying out acts of sabotage. They weren't perfect and they had their less enthusiastic moments but when they were centred on Christ there was something extremely winsome about their fervent faith that I have rarely encountered back in the West. We were shown a faith that stood up under great tests, providing an example that continues to help us consider our own trials that are often trivial inconveniences in comparison to theirs (*A Clearing of the Mists, 2016, p.144).

[32] Boxall asks whether people in minority (and sometimes persecuted) situations could perhaps be in a position to be able to "name" Babylon in "her present incarnation, and to receive encouragement and nourishment in their struggle from the apocalyptic vision" (Boxall, I, 2001, *Studies in the Book of Revelation,* p.59). Scholer adds that "any conflict anywhere and at anytime which tests and challenges the church and believers can and should be read against the historical and theological grid of Revelation" (Scholer, D.M., 2001, *Breaking the Code: Interpretive Reflections on Revelation, in Evangelical Review of Theology 25:4, p. 316).*

[33] Quoted from R Mark Walker: 2003, *Hope and Encouragement for the Oppressed; the Perspective of the Apocalypse of John on the Crises Facing its First Readers,* page1.

[34] As quoted by Peterson, E.H., 1969, *in Theology Today,* vol. 26, no. 2, p. 141.

[35] Ibid, p.140.

[36] So Schüssler Fiorenza, 1985, *The Book of Revelation: Justice & Judgment,* p.1. Susan White adds that: "Because of all the trouble it has caused, some of us would just rather pretend that the Book of Revelation isn't there in our Bibles at all. Since whatever truth it contains seems to be encoded in such complex symbolic and metaphorical language, perhaps it would be safer to wait until the Second Coming and then ask Jesus Christ himself what it is all about!" (1998, *Hope in Expository Times 109, no 7, April* p.212).

Gathercole, plus a scholar who had written his own book on Revelation. I had prepared a mountain of written answers, hoping to be able to use them to respond to the inevitable questions that would follow. "We're just going to have a wee chat. Set all your papers down on the floor over there," said the lecturer. Yeah, sure; they were here to grill me! Everything went really well and I was able to answer all the questions fired at me during the 1¼ hour exam, remembering things I'd read months ago and even managing a quotation from a gem of a book by Richard Bauckham.[37] The examiners even played "devil's advocate" at one point to see if I would spot the deliberate mistake. Thankfully I was able to correct their error in no uncertain terms! One of the scholar's comments is worth repeating; he thought the thesis was "very spiritual!" I don't think he meant it as a compliment but I certainly took it that way! Afterwards I was able to phone my lead supervisor from the International Christian College in Glasgow, Dr Stephen Chester, with the good news that I'd passed![38]

We all learn through such experiences and I was quick to adapt some of them into the classes at Chiguata. The students now had to also defend their assignments which were presented to the class orally, followed by questions and answers.

THE PASSION OF THE CHRIST

It was very enjoyable working with Jeff and Eric, both from the US. I think it was Jeff and I who decided to take all the students and staff to watch Mel Gibson's controversial movie *The Passion of the Christ*. It was in one of the top cinemas in Arequipa, quite a contrast for

---

[37] Bauckham R, 1993 *The Theology of the Book of Revelation.*
[38] I graduated *in absentia* on 28th January, 2004.

most of the *hermanos,* whose previous cinematic experiences would have been in the open air, in their local communities, as mentioned in chapter 7. The movie is, of course, Mel Gibson's interpretation of our Saviour's crucifixion, depicted in graphic detail (he produced, co-wrote and directed the film). One critic wrote the following:

A brutal moving and eye opening depiction of what Jesus endured to pay for our sins...It is an amazing film. It sucked me in completely...Of course we have the torture of Christ. Yes it was brutal and difficult to watch...Was it effective? Yes. Was it necessary? As a ...Christian I say...definitely...His film made me understand on a gut-wrenching, emotional level, what an enormous sacrifice Jesus made for mankind...it evoked a vision of the level of suffering that Christ endured...It was an affirmation and strengthening of my faith.[39]

We all agreed with Holtreman, returning to our respective homes, very touched and moved by our Saviour's love and incredible sacrifice. Surely the crucifixion was the greatest ever example of a stunningly, selfless act of compassion that the world has ever known. The physical aspects were horrendous; the mockery, the scoffing, the abuse, the spitting, the crown of thorns twisted together, the beatings, the nails, the extreme searing, agonising pain of the cross itself. A doctor, writing in the *Journal of the American Medical Association* explained the pain that would have been experienced in death by crucifixion:

Adequate exhalation required lifting the body by pushing up on the feet and by flexing the elbows...However, this manoeuvre would place the entire weight of the body on the tarsals and would produce searing pain. Furthermore, flexion of the elbows would cause rotation of the wrists about the iron nails and cause fiery pain along

---

[39] Vic Holtreman, 2004, *Screen Rant review.*

the damaged median nerves...Muscle cramps and paresthesias of the outstretched and uplifted arms would add to the discomfort. As a result, each respiratory effort would become agonising and tiring and lead eventually to asphyxia. [40]

In some cases, writes Grudem, "Crucified men would survive for several days, nearly suffocating but not quite dying. This was why the executioners would sometimes break the legs of a criminal, so that death would come quickly, as we see in John 19:31-33... Crucifixion was one of the most horrible forms of execution ever devised by man." [41]

Added to the physical pain Jesus went through, was the spiritual cost of bearing the guilt for our sins. Jesus was perfectly holy. He hated sin and evil as the Gospels portray so clearly. He was totally pure, innocent, perfect, the spotless Lamb of God. Yet, in obedience to the Father, and out of love for us, He took on Himself all the sin of the world. As Peter states in his 1st epistle, chapter 2:

He himself bore our sins in his body on the tree, so that we might die to sins and live for righteousness; by his wounds you have been healed (v. 24).

And again in chapter 3, verse 18:

For Christ died for sins once for all, the righteous for the unrighteous, to bring you to God.

We will never fully know just how much that incredible act of redemption cost our Lord as He suffered alone on the cross. We will never know, in this life anyway, exactly what He went through,

---

[40] William Edwards, March 21, 1986, *Journal of the American Medical Association, vol. 255, no 11*, p.1461.
[41] Wayne Grudem, 1994, *Systematic Theology, An Introduction to Biblical Doctrine*, p.573.

exactly what was involved. But Jesus did. In the Garden of Gethsemane, Scripture says that he was deeply distressed and troubled. He knew what lay ahead:

"My soul is overwhelmed with sorrow to the point of death," he said to them. "Stay here and keep watch." "Father, if you are willing, take this cup from me; yet not my will, but yours be done." An angel from heaven appeared to him and strengthened him. And being in anguish, he prayed more earnestly, and his sweat was like drops of blood falling to the ground (Mk. 14:32-34; Lk.22:42-44).

I attended an excellent school in Northern Ireland as a boarder. One of the advantages of this meant I could commit entirely to the educational and sporting facilities on offer (I thoroughly enjoyed playing both rugby and cricket). One of the disadvantages was the strict rules applied after lights out in the dormitories. Conversation of any kind was strictly forbidden after 10.30 pm. We were just young boys at the time so it was only natural to whisper to my mate to see if he'd heard the football results or something similar. Suddenly a voice rang out: "Talkers out. To my study – now!" Discipline in those days was somewhat different to what it is now – three on the behind using a gym slipper! So we arrived at the teacher's office expecting just that. However, on this occasion he simply told us to return to his office after school the next day. "Yahoo," we whooped at each other on the way back to the dormitories. But that exuberance soon disappeared as reality sank in; the punishment had merely been postponed. Come 3.30pm the following day, we would be back in his office!

That night I couldn't get to sleep. What lay ahead for me was constantly on my mind, the punishment awaiting. At breakfast I wasn't hungry. During the classes, I couldn't focus properly. Finally, after what seemed like an eternity, the hour arrived for us to go and receive the punishment. We left the office somewhat relieved, if not with rather sore bums!

I was guilty. I'd broken the rules. I deserved to be punished, albeit in a less physical manner. But Jesus didn't. He was innocent, pure, and perfect. He didn't break any rules. He didn't deserve to die. And yet He did, knowing what was to come; the agony, the humiliation, the searing pain. He could so easily have avoided it. But instead, He lay down His life as a living sacrifice for our sins, the righteous for the unrighteous, to bring us to God (1 Pet.3:18). Now there is hope instead of sadness, truth instead of lies and deception, love instead of hatred, light instead of darkness, life instead of death. He asks us to remember that ultimate sacrifice that gives hope to all humankind (1 Cor. 11:23-25). We did just that on the bus home from the cinema, each one quietly reflecting on the horrors we had just seen, offering up renewed prayers of thankfulness to our beloved Lord and Saviour.

NIGHT BIBLE INSTITUTES (NBI's) & HOME CHURCH

I was also invited to teach in two of the IEP's Night Bible Institutes in Arequipa, in the central church called La Merced and in Alto Cayma. I noticed straight away, in both places, that there was a very high standard of education and learning among the students. In La Merced we had quite a number of University graduates, engineers, teachers etc. The church President attended, as did some of the old hands whose knowledge of the Bible certainly kept me on my toes! One older student in particular stood out; *hermano* Lionel, who would go on to be the only one of my students to ever obtain a mark of 19 out of 20, 95%. Incidentally, I felt it necessary to cover over the names on the examination papers to avoid being influenced in any way when it came to marking. I then adopted a technique used by my old Latin teacher who would hand back the exam papers to all but the top ten, and then publicly announce who finished in 10th position, ninth position, right up to the best student in the class. I never did get to experience the excitement of being in the top ten for Latin, but it certainly worked a treat in the NBI's!

I taught this group two courses; New Testament Studies and Advanced Homiletics. In the latter course I handed round various items to be used for illustrative purposes in the sermons. The one item I remember handing out was a chocolate tin, shaped in the form of a heart. I had used this previously in the early days at Bible College, preaching to the sand dunes (chapter 3)![42] My take on it was to talk about the outside; how beautiful the tin looked, the lovely colour of the roses, the beautiful shape and all that the heart represents. Then I would tap it, open it up and show that it was practically useless because it was empty; there was nothing inside. The Biblical application was then applied, based on firstly Mark chapter 7 and Jesus' interaction with the Pharisees and His quotation from Isaiah 29:13:

"These people honour me with their lips, but their hearts are far from me.

They worship me in vain; their teachings are but rules taught by men."

Galatians 5:22-23 was also used, along with 1 Sam16:7:

But the Lord said to Samuel, "Do not consider his appearance or his height, for I have rejected him. The Lord does not look at the things

---

[42] The homiletics lecturer actually asked to borrow the tin to use for one of his talks!

man looks at. Man looks at the outward appearance, but the Lord looks at the heart. "

After this, I would remove some chocolates from my pocket, put them inside, stuff one into my mouth (with the appropriate exclamations of *"¡Oh qué rico!")* and offer the rest around the class! I can't remember their take on it, but I can remember the excitement and joy at being able to present a message in such a powerful, meaningful way.

The group in Alto Cayna, 32 in total, were just as rewarding to teach. This was definitely the younger generation; under graduates studying full time at University, others having just completed their day's work. Again the level was very high, though no one managed to top Lionel! The participation of the students was incredible; I only had to ask a question to set them off! The difficulty was trying to keep the lesson on track!

As another missionary was working in my previous church of *San Martín,* we decided to attend another Quechua church close by, *La Tomilla.* The Presbytery also asked if I could help in another fellowship as well, *Cuidad de Dios,* 40 minutes from Arequipa by bus. As so often happens in Peru, there was a problem regarding the title deeds to the *La Tomilla* church. The present owner's Dad, who had passed away, had allowed the church to be built on his property. Unfortunately, no legal deeds had been obtained and the father's children now wanted to use the ground for themselves. It's a pity that our friend, Pastor Alejandro Chara, also a solicitor and later a director of a Christian school, hadn't been involved in the original transaction. But we got him involved now and, with payment made to the family, everything was sorted out. Sadly, we heard recently he had passed away. He will be greatly missed.

One of the teenagers in the church had a bad accident involving his leg. We knew his parents really well, as they were both very involved in the ministry. Unfortunately, there is no NHS in Peru and while there are some free services available, they can vary in standard and quality. The family decided to pay for a doctor to carry out the operation, using up their hard earned financial resources. Sadly the operation was a disaster. It looked like the boy would never walk properly again. One morning "Andrea" knocked on our door, burst into tears and told us the whole story. We immediately got in touch with, firstly, a well known Christian doctor, and secondly, Betty Barrie from the Women's Fellowship at ABC. The ladies agreed to pay a donation towards the costs with ourselves making up the difference. This time the operation was a huge success, the doctor putting the necessary metal splints in the leg. The next time we saw their son he was playing volley ball! But the story doesn't ends there. "Andrea" insisted on returning to our house to work to pay off our part of the donation, which she did faithfully over the months ahead. We're all one big Christian family, here to help each other out in times of difficulty. And on home assignment, at the aforementioned Women's Fellowship meeting in our church, we were able to tell of the joy, hope and happiness their donation had brought.

VIOLETA'S MINISTRY

Violeta was also kept busy with both family and work, helping out with the *Liga* (Women's Fellowship) and the youth group in our church. The ladies met every Tuesday and after a short time of handicrafts, ceramics, knitting etc, would enjoy singing hymns in Quechua and Spanish and listening to the word of God. Vio was involved in both parts of the meeting, teaching ceramics and then bringing a message. As advisor to the *Liga,* she was able to help plan the programme, inviting former members along, organising all night prayer meetings, health talks, social aid etc. Planning was also required for the Presbytery conventions, not least in the provision of food for the many people who attended.

We also helped (Vio particularly) in the orientation programme for a lovely, recently arrived couple, Latin Link missionaries, Mirjam and Jürg Hofer. The folk today have a wonderful ministry in Trujillo, helping with *Corazones Unidos con Personas con Discapacidad* (United Hearts with People with Disabilities), an organisation helping people with difficulties in the various churches. Jürg is also the Pastor for the ministry supporting people with disabilities in their local church and Mirjam is the Peru Team Leader. And with my past experiences with "Project Timothy," it was only natural to have other people stay with us, taking part wherever possible, such as Dan McGowan and Martin Blewett (and later his wife Rosanna) in Cusco. Martin had brought his puppets with him, which went down really well everywhere we went.

There seemed to be a constant flow of people in and out of the house; Peruvian brothers and sisters, missionary colleagues including Kathryn, Ruth, Sarah, Carolyn, Marion, Esme and Tina; and of course family. Violeta's sister Carmen visited occasionally, as well as her brother Herzón. We were able to have a lovely short seaside break with Mum and Dad Alarcón Altamirano in the mission house in Mejía. Tía Lida also paid a visit, bringing a young girl to help look after Greg. It was great to be able to catch up with Javier, Betty and Favio once again as well.

GREGCITO

Greg was having a great time, making lots of friends firstly at a play group called *Garabatos* (scribbles). Inevitability, there were lots of games, painting, parades (he really looked the part dressed up in his Quechua clothing!), and the inevitable Nativity play (Greg appearing as Joseph) and graduation ceremony. Later, he went on to enjoy his time at nursery, in the *Colegio Internacional*. Again there were lots of wonderful social and academic events, many helping to raise funds for the school, providing a great opportunity for interaction with other parents and families. We reconnected with many former friends including my Spanish teachers Pedro (also a Pastor) and Julio (a dentist)! Enormous effort is put in to these events, setting up all kinds of stalls and activities, with fabulous local dishes on offer, such as different types of *tallarines* (noodle/pasta dishes) and *parilladas* (BBQ's). Arequipa, one of the gastronomic capitals of Peru, offers up some incredibly delicious dishes, such as *rocoto relleno* (noted for its striking colour and presentation, not forgetting its very soft texture and delicious mix of spicy and cheesy flavours. It consists of large hot Peruvian peppers stuffed with ground beef, onions, garlic, olives, raisins, herbs and spices, all topped off with fried cheese and baked in an egg and milk sauce). Another favourite is *Adobo de Chancho (Adobo Arequipeño),* a traditional soupy pork stew, slow simmered and marinated in *chicha de jora* (corn beer), spicy rocoto pepper, *ají panca,* (Peruvian red pepper), garlic, onions, oregano, cumin and other herbs and spices. As the meat is cooked all day in a clay pot, it literally falls off the bone. It is always served with bread, needed to dunk in to capture every last drop!

A range of flavoursome deserts were also on offer, including *buñuelos,* similar to fried doughnuts and served with a delicious sweet topping. With such a variety on offer it was impossible to sample everything. Thankfully, bags were provided for takeaways so the food could be enjoyed the next day! I think you'll realise by now my deep passion and love for Peruvian food!

We also met up with Dionicio and Bertha, whose youngest son Matt was in his final year. They invited us along to the school's presentation of the traditional Andean dance from Bolivia, the *Saya Caporal,* which Matt was participating in. It was a sensational evening; the boys and girls stunning in their traditional costumes, the music loud, vibrant and poignant, the movement and dancing perfect and precinct. They must have been practising for months for the whole ensemble moved together as one, in precise harmony. After the finale, the packed auditorium exploded into rapturous applause and cheering that seemed to never end. We were all filled with pride and joy for all the dancers, and for "little" Matt in particular.

Birthday parties are very big social events in Peru, especially for the children. The house would be packed with Greg's friends and parents, family members and others invited for the big celebration. As usual, the house would be suitably decorated, decked out in masses of balloons and banners. Clowns were hired to keep the kids amused. And of course there would be the inevitable food, birthday cake and *piñata,* a decorative figure made out of a container filled with sweets, fruits and toys which was covered with paper mache. Each child took it in turn to be blindfolded and to hit the figure with a stick. When the *piñata* finally broke open, everyone rushed forward to grab as many of the treats as they could!

SPIRITUAL WARFARE

These were some of the happiest days of our lives. However, not everything ran smoothly. In the midst of my course preparation for Chiguata (on the book of Revelation), when I was really getting excited at how the course was developing, things came dramatically to an abrupt halt. Poor Greg had an accident and had to be rushed to the nearby clinic. Within 45 minutes one of the best doctors in Arequipa was on hand to stitch up a deep gash. It could have been so much worse. I sensed we had been spiritually attacked by the enemy yet again.

When I was about two years old, I fell out of a first floor window. There is still a dent on my head to prove it. About a year later I almost died of pneumonia; the doctor saying to Mum and Dad that there was nothing more he could do. A little bit older, I tried to be Tarzan, swinging from branch to branch. Whatever happened, the branch slipped out of my hands and I landed flat on my back. The wind was literally taken out of me and I couldn't breathe for about twenty seconds. I thought I was a goner. On another occasion, while walking in to work, immediately after passing the barber's shop in Carrick Street, Ayr, there was a massive crash. The extremely heavy red and white stripped barber's sign had fallen on to the ground. If I'd been two seconds earlier, it would have landed right on top of my head. On another occasion, my friend David Craig invited me to speak at a Scripture Union camp at Barcaple, in the rolling hills of Dumfries and Galloway, close to Castle Douglas. It was a really enjoyable weekend which, I thought at the time, ended badly, as one of the car's tyres was flat (this delayed my departure by about 30 minutes). However, on the return journey home, I came across a car crash. Thankfully, there was nobody badly injured and I was able to continue on my journey shortly afterwards. Then I sensed the Holy

Spirit speaking to me and reminding me about the puncture. If I had left 30 minutes earlier, my car would have been involved in the accident.

Yes, spiritual warfare does exist. We live in a fallen world, a world that lives in darkness, separated from God. Satan uses every tactic possible to blind people from the good news of the Gospel. It says in 2 Corinthians 4:4 that:

The god of this age has blinded the minds of unbelievers, so that they cannot see the light of the gospel of the glory of Christ, who is the image of God.

He uses every tactic possible to keep them in bondage to things that hinder them from coming to God (Gal.4:3, 8), bondage to sexual immorality, idolatry, impurity, greed, obscenity, foolish talk, coarse joking etc. Satan has his own realm and kingdom as Luke, Paul and John make very clear:

The devil led him up to a high place and showed him in an instant all the kingdoms of the world. And he said to him, "I will give you all their authority and splendour, for it has been given to me, and I can give it to anyone I want to..." (Lk. 4:5-6).

For he has rescued us from the dominion of darkness and brought us into the kingdom of the Son he loves, in whom we have redemption, the forgiveness of sins (Col. 1:13-14).

We know that we are children of God, and that the whole world is under the control of the evil one (1 Jn. 5:19).

Just as God has His kingdom in this world with its members (you and me!), so Satan also has his. Satan's spirit, as it says in Ephesians 2:1-

2, *"is at work in those who are disobedient."* The devil, writes Paul in 2 Timothy 2:26, *"has taken them captive to do his will."*

And not only does he have his own realm, kingdom and authority, he also has power as Luke states in Acts 26:17b-18:

I am sending you to them to open their eyes and turn them from darkness to light, and from the power of Satan to God, so that they may receive forgiveness of sins and a place among those who are sanctified by faith in me.

The Bible also describes Satan as prowling around like a roaring lion looking for someone to devour (1 Pet. 5:8). He works constantly against the Christian (his very name means "adversary" or "enemy,") using temptation, doubt, guilt, fear, confusion, sickness, envy, pride, slander and other means to hinder our witness, usefulness, relationship or communion with God. Satan will do anything and everything to hinder us, to make life more difficult for us, to get us down, to nullify our faith, our effectiveness, our work and ministry for the Lord.

But let me assure you of something that the Bible makes very clear. Satan has been defeated. Christ triumphed over him on the cross, as John states in the book of Revelation, chapter 5, verses 9-10:

"You are worthy to take the scroll and to open its seals, because you were slain, and with your blood you purchased men for God from every tribe and language and people and nation. You have made them to be a kingdom and priests to serve our God, and they will reign on the earth."

Christ is also presently at the right hand of God, interceding for us (Rom. 8:34, 1 Tim. 2:5, Heb. 7:25, 1 Jn. 2:1). As Paul writes in 2 Tim. 4:18:

The Lord will recue me from every evil attack and will bring me safely to his heavenly kingdom.

God's angels are also with us, protecting us, as Psalm 34:7 states:

The angel of the Lord encamps around those who fear him, and he delivers them (see also Gen.19:1, 10-11; 2 Kg.6:15-17; Ps.91:11). Hebrews 1:14 adds:

Are not all angels ministering spirits sent to serve those who will inherit salvation?

And what about the following verses:

Those who are with us are more than those who are with them (2 Kg.6:16-17; when the eyes of Elisha's servant were opened and he saw the hills full of horses and chariots of fire).

If God is for us, who can be against us? (Rom.8:31).

We are more than conquerors (Rom.8:37).

You, dear children, are from God and have overcome them, because the one who is in you is greater than the one who is in the world (1 Jn. 4:4).

Resist the devil, and he will flee from you. Come near to God and he will come near to you (Jm.4:7-8).

As I've mentioned previously, the Bible uses various phrases and expressions to describe Christians. We are the children of light (Ef.5:8, Ph.2:14-15), the sons and daughters of the living God. We are the children of God (Jn.1:12-13, Gal.3:26 ff., 1Jn.3:1), the people of God (Titus 2:14, 1 Pet.2:10, 3:18), *"a chosen people, a royal priesthood, a holy nation, a people belonging to God"* (1 Pet.2:9). A special relationship exists between us and God. We have been elevated beyond our sometimes seemingly insignificant human existence to another realm, the spiritual realm of God. Spiritual birth has occurred which brings us into intimate relationship with God as His children. Just as physical birth endows the newborn with a special relationship with his or her parents, so also our spiritual birth means we are sons and daughters of God and members of His family. Through regeneration, in the moment of being born again, we have received the infusion of divine life.

It's a bit like the infusion that occurs in a *mate* (hot herbal drink). When the fresh herbs or bags are added to the boiling water, there is a reaction, a change. The water is not the same as it was before. It changes colour, taste and essence. It's good, it's delicious and it's healthy! And, in a sense, that's what happens to us. There is a permanent infusion of God's divine presence that changes us. We become new creations (2 Cor.5:17), receiving spiritual life. We develop a genuine love for God, His people and everyone in the world. We develop Christ like character traits that Paul calls the fruit of the Spirit which become more and more evident in us; things like love, joy, peace, patience, kindness, goodness, faithfulness, gentleness and self-control (Gal.5:22-23). The Holy Spirit enables us to live lives free of continual sin, with the ability to overcome the pressures and temptations of the world. This does not mean that we will have perfect lives and live as saints. It does mean that the pattern of life will not be one of continuing indulgence to sin. Our bodies are temples of the Holy Spirit which results in behavioural changes and desires that are pleasing to God. We now have more trust and assurance of our forgiveness. We have a desire to read the Bible and to pray. We delight in worshipping the King of kings; indeed, we have a need to praise and thank Him. We have a desire to tell others about Jesus. We have received the breath of God and the implantation of

His divine nature, by means of the Holy Spirit who lives within us. We are God's spiritual children, the spiritual offspring of God. We belong to a kingdom that is much more powerful and much more glorious than any mere earthly kingdom. We belong to the kingdom of God.

And His presence is always with us during the good and bad times. Life is not an easy path for any of us. Scripture says that we all have waters to pass through, rivers to cross and fires to walk through (Is.43:1-3). Yet it also tells us that God will always be with us during these times; the waters will not sweep over us, nor will the flames set us ablaze. We are precious and honoured in His sight (v. 4). He loves us so much, commanding His angels to guard us in all our ways (Ps. 91:9-16).

BACK IN THE UK

We returned to the UK for good on the 17th May, 2005, with mixed feelings and memories that would last forever. Greg soon settled into a local primary school, with Vio and I taking over the running of the gift shop as well as working in an after school club (Violeta). Our journey continued with church involvement, the Lay Preacher's Association, business and family life and various visits to Peru over the years.

Greg would go on to secondary school, playing for Ayr rugby club and his school, as well as football, again for both a local team and school (in goals). One of the highlights was his participation in the school play, Calamity Jane. He remembered all his lines and excelled with his southern US drawl! He is presently at Uni, studying law.

When I look back I wonder how on earth it was all possible. How was I able to serve the Lord in such a way and, hopefully, accomplish things for His glory and His kingdom? The answer lies, of course, not through earthly ability, but through divine empowering, anointing, enablement and guidance. Surely the sceptic couldn't say it was all coincidence; almost every page of this book permeates with the inevitable fact that the living God is at work, active, actually present. These are not coincidences; they are God's incidents, part and parcel of His plans for my life.[43] When I took part in an evangelistic campaign in a place called *Punto de Bonbón*, relatively close to *Mejía,* on the Arequipeñan coast, I talked to a lady about her relationship with the Lord. "How do you stand before God?" I asked her. The reply was that she belonged to such and such a church. "Fine" I said, "Do you read your Bible each day and pray to God?" The answer was the same; she belonged to a particular church. "Okay. Do you have a personal relationship with the living God?" I think you can guess the answer; she belonged to that church. It's not about that I tried to tell her. It's not about belonging to a club or to a particular church. It's all about your personal relationship with the heavenly Father.

A good friend of mine was quite a rebel in his former days; long hair, motor bikes, heavy metal etc. Yet no one, absolutely no one, knew the Bible better than him! He once told me how he was at a meeting in an auditorium when an extremely well dressed man approached his row. My friend sent up an arrow prayer to God: "Lord, if he sits beside me, I'm going to ask him if he's been born again." Sure enough the man sat down beside him and my friend asked his question. The man looked at him in disgust and said: "Born again, that's all you people ever talk about!" The approach was probably a little direct to say the

---

[43] I first heard this phrase when Debbie Meehan (Southside Christian Fellowship), preached at Partick Baptist Church, Glasgow. It was part of the practical side of the Homiletics course I was helping to teach in our local church.

least. But when he told me the story, it reminded me of the chocolate tin illustration. It's the inside that matters!

I once visited quite a remote village near Cusco called Umachurco. Getting there involved a short drive, followed by a two hour trek into the mountains. After the service I noticed one of the *hermanos* standing alone, looking totally dejected. So I went over for a chat and found out that his self-esteem was rock bottom, he felt so insignificant and useless. *"Hermano,"* I asked him. "In the eyes of the world, who is the most important person on this earth?" "The President of The USA," he replied. It was, however, at a time when the President had been accused of being involved in a scandal. While this may have been the case, and while it was not correct for me to judge anyone, I thought it proper to ask the following question. "In the eyes of God *hermano,* who is He more pleased with; you, or the President of the USA?" "Me, *hermano* Marcos." A massive smile lit up his face as he realised the significance of his answer. He might appear to be relatively insignificant in the eyes of the world, but to His heavenly Father, that was not the case. He was a special person, a child of God, a born again son of the living, Holy Father.

Jesus, in his very own words tells us that "no-one can see the kingdom of God unless he is born again...born of water and the Spirit" (Jn.3:3-8). We "reflect the Lord's glory" and are being "transformed into his likeness with ever-increasing glory, which comes from the Lord, who is the Spirit" (2 Cor. 3:18). It is all about a personal relationship with the living God. I talk to Him every day, sometimes crying out in times of need and desperation. I sing praises to His name; in the shower, washing the dishes, driving in the car. I would never have made it on my own. I could not and cannot live without Him. I praise God each day that I belong to Him, that I am a Christian, born of the Spirit of God. I'm so glad that Jesus loves me. I'm so honoured and blessed to have a personal relationship, little old, insignificant me, with the maker of heaven and earth, and of the universe, the Lord, God Almighty. I'm so glad that I'm not alone, ever. Thank goodness the heavenly Father understands me, putting up with my bad days! Thank goodness for His amazing grace and forgiveness. Praise the Lord for the light that shines within me, the fruit of which produces goodness, righteousness and truth (Eph.5:8-9). Thank goodness for His empowering and anointing. Thank goodness for that little small voice that talks to me and guides me. And thank goodness that His divine presence, in the form of the Holy Spirit, lives within me (1Cor.3:16 etc.). Let me say that again, the Spirit of Him who raised Jesus from the dead, the Spirit of God, lives within you and within me. Isn't that astounding! Isn't that amazing! Isn't that awesome! He gives divine life to our mortal bodies (Rom.8:11). He strengthens us with power (Eph.3:16). And like any good earthly parent, He takes our hands and gently leads and directs us. Yes, let us sing at the top of our voices, Philip P Bliss's wonderful hymn "Jesus loves even me":

I am so glad that Jesus loves me,

Jesus loves me, Jesus loves me.

I am so glad, that Jesus loves me,

Jesus loves even me.

CHAPTER 12

The Journey Continues;
A Conclusion

A Scottish *haar* is a weather phenomenon which occurs in spring and summer, when warm air passes over the cold North Sea, resulting in condensation. Very small particles of water are then suspended in the air, forming a thick, cold, dense fog.

We live in Ayr, 37 miles south west of Glasgow. It is the birthplace to Scotland's national bard, Robert Burns. It is also a popular seaside resort, with beautiful walks along the esplanade and sandy beach, which offers fabulous views of the beautiful Isle of Arran. This island, the largest in the Firth of Clyde, is often called "Scotland in miniature," due to the stunning scenery, wonderful wildlife and its wide range of outdoor activities. One such favourite of ours is to take the ferry across from Ardrossan to Brodick, walk along the beach to the base of Goatfell, then climb the island's highest peak (approximately 874 metres high, 2866 feet), before returning to Brodick in time for some fish and chips and the evening ferry home!

Hebrews 11:1 gives us a good definition of what faith is:

Now faith is being sure of what we hope for and certain of what we do not see

Some time ago, our youth worker, Samuel Yawila from Zambia, preached on this verse and on the need to have faith in God, even when we cannot literally see Him. I've never forgotten the illustration Samuel used to emphasise this reality and truth. In his time in Ayr, as he walked along the beach, he too had looked over to the beautiful Isle of Arran, the mountains resplendent in the sunshine during the day, or gleaming in the stunning sunsets the area is famous for. But this is not always the case. He mentioned experiencing his first *haar,* when the island appeared to literally disappear, becoming invisible due to the thick, dense sea fog. He said that despite not being able to actually see Arran, only a fool would say that it was no longer there, that it didn't exist. He then went on to apply this to faith and the need to be 100% certain and sure of all the wonderful promises in the Bible including God's presence and touch upon our lives. It is often difficult to see through the fog of this world and beyond the challenges of this life. Faith is the fuel of the Christian life, making us certain of all these things. Without it, it is impossible to please God. We must believe that He exists and that He rewards those who earnestly seek Him (Heb.11:6).

As Paul adds in 2 Cor.5:7:

We live by faith, not by sight.

What a wonderful, powerful way to illustrate what faith involves; the need to believe that God is always there, always present, always out there, even when it doesn't appear so. No matter what we are going through, no matter what crisis we are experiencing, we are never, ever alone.

GUIDANCE THROUGH SCRIPTURE

I hope this book has encouraged you in your faith, as you have seen God at work in my life. He is not some distant impersonal deity who we dare not speak to or even mention by name. No, He is totally the opposite. He takes us by the hand and leads us through life's journey, day, after day, after day, providing divine guidance. It is very likely that guidance will come through Scripture or the preaching of the word which is living and active, God breathed, like fire, sharper than any double edged sword, able to penetrate deep, deep into our hearts and souls. That word is so powerful that it can bring even the toughest of men to their knees in tears of repentance. It is a lamp to our feet and a light for our paths. He knows the plans He has for us and instructs us and teaches us in the way we should go. Let's prioritise our quiet times as a means of soaking in the word of God, of absorbing His divine presence and of hearing His voice. God reveals Himself fully to us in the Bible – His nature, Presence, promises and love. The spoken word of God has supernatural power to build faith in its readers and listeners. We must always find time each day to immerse ourselves in it, even during the busiest of times. Lets also prioritise listening to the preaching of the word; God can guide and speak to us through it. People can be used prophetically by God, to convey His message to us.

GUIDANCE THROUGH OTHER PEOPLE

Guidance may come through conversing with others, listening to the advice particularly from mature godly Christians who we respect and look up to, such as our parents, pastors or friends. It is normal practice for the preacher or speaker to go to the door after the service or meeting to shake hands with the people. Don't be afraid to share with the person whatever is on your heart. The words they say to us can again be used by God to penetrate deep; challenging, moving and directing us. Also listen to people's requests. Remember the knock on the door in chapter 10? That unexpected visit, totally out of the blue, and the subsequent conversation, opened up a door to an incredible ministry. Pray for God to speak to you or to use you to speak to others. Be a Barnabas! Keep your ears open! Listen to what He is saying.

GUIDANCE THROUGH THE HOLY SPIRIT AND TIMES OF SILENCE

It may be through the work of the Holy Spirit who is able to speak, to lead, to guide, to direct, to light the way. Don't forget to have moments of quietness, times to listen and to receive direction from that still, small voice of the Lord, that gentle whisper, as in Elijah's case. Listen out for that whisper in your life, even if it comes in the middle of the night. And always look out for little "coincidences," especially when the timing is spot on. We must be open to the living God working in His church today. Yield to His gentle touch; be sensitive to His prompting.

GUIDANCE THROUGH PRAYER

And we all know the importance of prayer and how powerful it is, helping us to cope with difficult situations and circumstances. We have all, no doubt, had to cry out to Him, asking for help in times of need. I had to do exactly that when working in the shop during the busy summer months while Violeta and Greg were in Peru visiting family. Unfortunately Greg became unwell and was diagnosed as having bird flu, which at the time, was lethal. They took x-rays, blood samples, gave him strong antibiotics and put him in a private room, all to no avail. His condition was deteriorating, the tablets weren't working and with the bird flu pandemic worsening, flying back to the UK, we were told, was not an option. The future was grim. Violeta's voice, when she phoned, was naturally full of fear and hysteria. What do you do in such a situation? What could I do so far away from my loved ones? I was helpless. And for a parent there is nothing worse than not being able to come to the assistance of your child, children, or family. The only thing I could do was cry out to God. I poured my heart out to Him, praying and fasting. The words of Hebrews 5:7 came to mind:

During the days of Jesus' life on earth, he offered up prayers and petitions with loud cries and tears to the one who could save him from death, and he was heard because of his reverent submission.

I shared my needs and concerns with the folk at Milestone Christian Fellowship who joined in prayer as well.[44] On the return journey from Girvan, I stopped the car in a lay-by near Dunure, with panoramic views out to the island of Arran. It brought back memories of Samuel's sermon. I knew God was present. I knew He was listening. So I handed the situation over to Him, immediately experiencing, for the first time in days, incredible peace of mind.

Meanwhile, Violeta went to the KLM office in Lima to see if the hospital was right about Greg not being allowed to fly. They confirmed this was the case but suggested getting a second opinion, recommending the doctor used by the KLM staff in Lima. They also pointed out that, due to the peak season, all the planes flying from Lima to Amsterdam were fully booked!

---

[44] Noel McCullins had since "retired" as Pastor from ABC but was soon involved as the networker for the Baptist churches in the region. One of his dreams was to re-establish the church in Girvan, which eventually came to fruition, with the church meeting in the community centre. Today Milestone Christian Fellowship has its own premises and is a thriving church under the care of Pastor Adam Oellermann and the leadership team.

Two things happened. Firstly, the doctor turned out to be a total blessing. "What are these x-rays for? I don't need them. Throw all those tablets away; they are useless. The boy doesn't have bird flu – he has pneumonia. All he needs is penicillin. He can return immediately to the UK on the next available plane." Wow! What an answer to prayer. But what about the next problem, trying to find space on a plane bound for Amsterdam, then on to Glasgow? Vio went back to the KLM office to find that there had just been a cancellation; two seats were available at the very back of the plane! Would she like to have them? *Hallelu Yah!* Praise the Lord! Thank you so much for your divine intervention.

When the folks appeared at the arrivals building, Greg didn't come running into my arms with a massive smile on his face as was his custom. Instead he sat in his buggy, white as a ghost, no smile whatsoever. But they were home. Greg was safe. Our own doctor confirmed the diagnosis as pneumonia and it wasn't long before the big fella was back on his feet. Thank you for your mercy Lord, for your goodness to us in our time of need. Thank you for hearing our cries and for your compassion, grace and love.

In some of the prayers in Scripture, we can almost hear the great intensity with which our brothers and sisters pour out their hearts to God. Daniel cries out:

Now, our God, hear the prayers and petitions of your servant...Give ear, O God, and hear; open your eyes and see...We do not make requests of you because we are righteous, but because of your great mercy. O Lord, listen! O Lord, forgive! O Lord, hear and act! (Dan.9:17-19).

When God shows Amos the judgment He is going to bring on His people, Amos pleads, crying out:

Sovereign Lord, forgive! I beseech you! How can Jacob survive? He is so small! (Amos 7:2).

And of course David, whose very life was threatened on numerous occasions, cried out the very words that our Saviour would use on the cross:

My God, my God, why have you forsaken me? Why are you so far from saving me, so far from the words of my groaning? O my God, I cry out by day, but you do not answer, by night, and am not silent (Ps.22:1-2).

Time and time again, we read of David's prayers from the heart, crying out in times of need, to his heavenly Father:

Have mercy on me, O God, have mercy on me, for in you my soul takes refuge. I will take refuge in the shadow of your wings until the disaster has passed. I cry out to God Most High, to God, who fulfils his purpose for me. He sends from heaven and saves me, rebuking those who hotly pursue me; God sends his love and his faithfulness (Ps. 57:1-3).

Out of the depths I cry to you, O Lord; O Lord, hear my voice. Let your ears be attentive to my cry for mercy (Ps.130:1-2).

Just like the writer of Psalm 88 who, going through incredibly difficult troubling times, opened his heart to God:

O Lord, the God who saves me, day and night I cry out before you. May my prayer come before you; turn your ear to my cry. For my soul is full of trouble and my life draws near the grave. I am counted among those who go down to the pit; I am like a man without strength...I call to you, O Lord, every day; I spread out my hands to you. ...I cry to you for help, O Lord; in the morning my prayer comes before you. (Ps. 88:1-4,9,13).

The writer of Lamentations, probably Jeremiah according to ancient Jewish and Christian tradition, in a time of severe crises, tells us to cry out in the night and to pour out our hearts like water in the presence of the Lord (2:19).

If we care about something or someone passionately, our prayers need to be passionate as well, coming from the heart. When we care and love people so much, it is only natural to pray with intense emotional involvement and to expect God, as a merciful Father, to respond to those heartfelt petitions. Scripture tells us that His ears are attentive to our cries for help (Ps.5:2-3, 34:15). David put his hope in the Lord and in His unfailing love and faithfulness (Ps.57:10, 130:5, 7). Time and time again, God lifted him out of the slimy pit, out of the mud and mire, setting his feet on a rock, creating stability, assurance and confidence. He put a new song in David's mouth, "a hymn of praise to our God" (Ps.40:1-3).

Never ever underestimate the power of prayer. Don't think you can solve all your problems by yourself. When you're in your darkest hour, in times of great need and want, don't rely solely on yourself. Instead rely on God. Fix your eyes on Him (2 Ch.20:12, Ps.25:15). Set your hope on the Father. He is merciful. He is compassionate. He is faithful. And He will deliver. He will provide! He loves you! Call out to Him in humility and reverent submission.

...Call upon me in the day of trouble; I will deliver you; and you will honour me (Psm.50:15).

We can pray in private, like Daniel who went to his upstairs room three times a day (Dan.6:10). Like Jesus, who often went out into solitary places to be alone with the Father (Lk.5:16 etc.), and who teaches:

...When you pray, go into your room, close the door and pray to your Father, who is unseen. Then your Father, who sees what is done in secret, will reward you (Mt.6:6).

Times alone with the Saviour help us to unscramble our thoughts, soothing out the day ahead, energising and empowering us. Go for a walk along the banks of a river or some other beautiful setting. Enjoy this special time, free from distraction and the busyness of life. Talk to the Father as you observe and soak in the wonders of nature, imbibing in the enchanting, breathtaking, stunning scenery. Sit out in your garden and do absolutely nothing. Take in the beauty all around – the sweet scent of the flowers in full bloom; the sound and sight of the birds toing and froing. Think of peaceful things – special times in your church or family life, wonderful holidays. Ask for stillness and peace. Ask for His intangible presence to move with you to face the day ahead.

We can also share our prayer needs with others as well, at a church meeting, in a house group or in prayer triplets (cf. Mt.18:19-20). Paul had to do just that, as he coped with incredible hardships and difficulties (2 Cor.11:23 ff.):

Indeed, in our hearts we felt the sentence of death. But this happened that we might not rely on ourselves but on God, who raises the dead. He has delivered us from such a deadly peril, and he will deliver us. On him we have set our hope that he will continue to deliver us, as you help us by your prayers. Then many will give thanks on our behalf for the gracious favour granted us in answer to the prayers of many (2 Cor.1:9-11).

Epaphras wrestled in prayer for the church in Colosse (Col.4:12). There is great strength and power in praying together, in sharing our burdens and sufferings. We help each other through our prayers, joining in the struggle and difficulty (Rom.15:30). Praying with others increases our faith and the effectiveness of our prayers.

And don't forget to use arrow prayers in moments of indecision and need, to ask for guidance and direction. Shoot off your prayers to heaven! Involve Him in the decision making process.

GUIDANCE THROUGH CORRECTION

Guidance sometimes takes the form of corrective action by God. Sadly we do not always walk in His ways, walking as Jesus did (1 Jn.2:6), living holy and honourable lives that are pleasing to Him. We need to control our bodies, displaying discipline and self control. We need to feed our spiritual nature, as opposed to the sinful nature, just like the two dogs illustration. We must refrain from a life pattern of continuous sin. If we don't, God may, on certain occasions, take actions to make our paths straight. These actions, I believe, will help us, in turn, to come closer to God and to learn to depend on Him more. The Psalmist appears to allude to this in chapter 119:71:

It was good for me to be afflicted so that I might learn your decrees.

It is important to state that not everything that happens to us is what God would want. God's will is not always done on earth; we don't always do it for example. Nor am I saying that God causes everything bad to happen. But He does permit certain things to happen. For example, God didn't throw Joseph into the cistern or sell him on to the Ismaelites when he went to check on his brothers near Shechem (Gen.37:12 ff.). But the Midianite merchants did take Joseph on to

Egypt, from where God was able to use him mightily. God didn't put Paul in prison, but He did allow that to happen. And when Paul was in prison, God used him to write huge chunks of the New Testament. Likewise, God didn't throw Daniel into the lion's den. But He allowed it to happen and through it brought great glory to His name, by means of the King's decree:

Then King Darius wrote to all the peoples, nations and men of every language throughout the land: "May you prosper greatly! I issue a decree that in every part of my kingdom people must fear and reverence the God of Daniel. For he is the living God and he endures for ever; his kingdom will not be destroyed, his dominion will never end. He rescues and he saves; he performs signs and wonders in the heavens and on the earth, He has rescued Daniel from the power of the lions" (Daniel 7:25-27).

Sometimes, God allows things to happen for His own will and purposes. And sometimes, He also has to take action as a means of making our paths straight and correcting our waywardness. Due to the filial relationship the Father has with us, and out of His love for us, there is a need for discipline:

"My son, do not make light of the Lord's discipline, and do not lose heart when he rebukes you, because the Lord disciplines those he loves, and he punishes everyone he accepts as a son" (Heb. 12:5-6).

Our fathers disciplined us for a little while as they thought best; but God disciplines us for our good, that we may share in his holiness. No discipline seems pleasant at the time, but painful. Later on, however, it produces a harvest of righteousness and peace for those who have been trained by it (Heb. 12:10-11; cf. Deut. 8:5, Prov. 3:11-12, Rev. 3:19-20).

"Does the Lord delight in burnt offerings and sacrifices as much as in obeying the voice of the Lord? To obey is better than sacrifice, and to heed is better than the fat of rams" (1 Sam.15:22).

We need to be humble and accept our discipline, as the writer of Proverbs 15 states:

He who listens to a life-giving rebuke will be at home among the wise. He who ignores discipline despises himself, but whoever heeds correction gains understanding. The fear of the Lord teaches a man wisdom, and humility comes before honour (Prov.15:31-33).

According to Proverbs, only fools despise wisdom and discipline (1:7, 12:1).

STEP OUT IN FAITH

If you've ever gone skiing in the Cairngorms, you've almost certainly been to Aviemore in the Scottish Highlands. It's a popular holiday resort, surrounded by breathtaking towering mountains and sparkling lochs. The air is as fresh as it gets! It is the home to stunning scenery and wonderful wildlife. It is also the home to the Landmark Forrest Adventure Park, which we once visited during the Easter holidays. There are so many activities going on; from the Runaway Timber Train to the Wild Water Coaster, from the Tree Top Trail to the Fire Tower, with amazing views from the UK's tallest wooden tower. And so much more! The highlight for us turned out to be the Sky Dive, described in the brochure as "beyond white knuckle, the ultimate dare, the ultimate achievement." It is basically a 15 metre (45 feet) pole which people step off and, by means of a harness, land gently onto the ground. We watched a young girl try to do it. Her family coaxed her. We coaxed her. The cable operator beside her coaxed her. Instead of standing up, she tried sitting down, hoping to just slide off. Nothing worked. Her face was contorted with fear. What do you think the harness operator did next? He crept up behind her and pushed her off! Within a second or two, the cable cut in and she glided gently to the ground. Then, after all the cheering and clapping, the biggest smile we'd ever seen flashed across her face!

Greg was eleven years old at the time, so I said to him: "Fancy a go at it son? If you do it, I'll follow straight after." The big fella climbed up the ladder, put the harness on as instructed, walked across the ledge and stepped straight off. Easy-peasy. Gulp. Now it was my turn. I climbed up the ladder, put the harness on, walked across the ledge, and looked down. Utter fear ran through me. From the ground 15 metres looks nothing, the pole seemed relatively small. But from up there it was a totally different story. Thoughts of climbing back down entered my head. I tried to jump off one side which didn't work. Finally, I plucked up the courage, stepped off and, with legs kicking everywhere in mid air in panic, landed on the ground. My heart was thumping. The instructor shouted down: "It's that step of faith, isn't it!"

Just like the harness and cable, which allowed for a safe descent and gentle landing from the Sky Dive, so too is God's almighty hand upon His people; upholding us, helping us to overcome, ever present with us in our difficult moments and tough times. The phrase "mighty hand," or "strong hand," is used in the Bible to describe God's incredible, miraculous power. For example, in the book of Exodus, the Lord said to Moses:

"Now you will see what I will do to Pharaoh: Because of my mighty hand he will let them go; because of my mighty hand he will drive them out of his country" (Ex.6:1).

The subsequent narrative goes on to illustrate just how powerful the hand of God is: a staff turned into a snake, the Nile's water turned to blood, there were animals, insects, storms and total darkness. The camel's back was finally broken when every Egyptian firstborn, both men and animals, were struck down (Ex.12:12). And in Chapter 13:3, Moses said to the people:

"Commemorate this day, the day you came out of Egypt, out of the land of slavery, because the Lord brought you out of it with a mighty hand."

Exodus 14 tells us what happened next; the Lord drove the sea back, the waters were parted and the Israelites walked across on dry land, with wells of water all around (Ex.14:22). Can you imagine actually being there, watching the waters divide then crossing over on dry land, with a massive well of water piled up to your right and to your left? Almost inconceivable; definitely mind-boggling! What a God! The Lord brought them out. The Lord rescued them. The Lord was with His people, fulfilling every promise He had made to them.

Later, as the Hebrews were on the verge of entering the promised land, Moses had this to say:

"O Sovereign Lord, you have begun to show to your servant your greatness and your strong hand. For what god is there in heaven or on earth who can do the deeds and mighty works you do?" (Dt.3:24).

The answer: there isn't one. No one else can do the mind-blowing deeds and mighty works of our God. Isn't that so assuring for the Christian; that despite the seriousness of the situation we are going through, no matter how difficult the problem may appear to be, to God it is nothing. With His help, with His strong hand, we too can overcome. He makes our steps firm; though we stumble, we will not fall; the Lord upholds us with His hand (Psm.37:23-24). We need to believe this! We need to take on board whole heartedly the wonderful promises the Bible contains! We need to never doubt or have unbelief (Heb.3:19). Instead we need to have tenacious faith, clinging firmly to the great hope the Gospel brings:

+- That God is present with us, always. We are never alone. He will never leave us or forsake us:

"Never will I leave you; never will I forsake you." So we say with confidence, *"The Lord is my helper; I will not be afraid. What can man do to me?"* (Heb.13:5-6).

*"Be strong and courageous. Do not be afraid or terrified because of them, for the Lord your God goes with you; he will **never** leave you nor forsake you"* (Duet.31:6).

+- That He has the power to do anything, absolutely anything.[45]

+- That He is our strength, our protector, our shield, our rock, our fortress, our stronghold, the horn of our salvation (Psm.18:1-2). He is also our shepherd, leading us, guiding us, providing for us and keeping us safe.

+- That we have an incredible, personal relationship with the living God:

"I will live with them and walk among them, and I will be their God, and they will be my people...I will be a Father to you, and you will be my sons and daughters, says the Lord Almighty" (2 Cor.6:16, 18).

---

[45] At Bible College we always had a time of prayer and praise before going out to share the Gospel. I always requested Kay Chance's chorus *"Ah Lord God."* The words are so poignant and powerful: *"Ah Lord God, Thou hast made the heavens and the earth by Thy great power. Ah Lord God, Thou hast made the heavens and the earth by Thine outstretched arm. Nothing is too difficult for Thee, nothing is too difficult for Thee, O great and mighty God; great in counsel and mighty in deed, nothing, nothing, absolutely nothing, nothing is too difficult for Thee."*

The hope for this world is found in that wonderful relationship that exists between God the Father and His people. Our sins have been forgiven; we have been brought from death to life (Rom.6:13).

+- That we have a wonderful future to look forward to; in His eternal presence for ever and ever:

For God so loved the world that he gave his one and only Son, that whoever believes in him shall not perish but have eternal life (Jn.3:16).

And we also need to put this faith into practice. We need to sometimes physically step off the ledge, taking that step of faith. The cable only functions when the person actually steps off the platform. God needs us to take that step of faith.

Most weekends at Bible College, teams of students were sent out to take part in church services, evangelistic meetings etc. We would always meet up beforehand to discuss our roles in the services; sometimes there would be both a morning and evening service to take. I was appointed team leader for one particular Sunday, and at the pre-event meeting the roles were shared out. One of the ladies would preach in the morning, I would share the message in the evening. Another brother would lead the morning service, sharing his testimony in the evening. But there was still one lady left. As I knew she loved working with children, I suggested she might like to give a children's talk in the morning. We all thought that was a good idea and finished the meeting. However, later on in the week, she approached me and said she couldn't do it; she had never done a children's talk before. I told her the College had an outreach library full of ready prepared messages especially for children. I also advised her to speak to one of the other female students who was highly expertise in this area. She was still hesitant, but I refused to budge.

We were part of a team going to serve the Lord together. Thanks to prayer, encouragement and the faith of that lady, when the time came for the children's talk, she stepped up and delivered one of the best presentations I had ever seen and heard! She had taken that step of faith, overcoming fear, doubt and worry.

In Mark chapter 4, we read about Jesus calming the storm. In the evening, as they travelled across the lake, a furious squall came up, the waves pouring into the boat, nearly swamping it. Jesus was fast asleep in the back! The disciples, many of whom were fishermen and accustomed to rough waters, were afraid and woke him up. Jesus, of course, rebuked the wind and waves, and everything returned to normal (vv.35-39). It is interesting Jesus' following question to them:

"Why are you so afraid? Do you still have no faith?" (v.40)

Fear caused the disciples to doubt. Some of them had already seen the Saviour at work, performing mighty miracles and driving out many demons in Capernaum and throughout Galilee (chps.1-3). Yet their faith, in this instance, was lacking. They did not believe in the protective hand of God, in His power, presence and promises. When the crunch came, they were found lacking. Someone once said that fear is the opposite of faith. David Hathaway goes further, stating that "spiritual warfare is not merely against the devil, it is also when you fight your own unbelief...Doubt is one of the devil's biggest weapons against believers."[46]

I want to encourage you to believe in yourself and in your ability and not to doubt. Maybe you're someone who has served the Lord faithfully over the years, not necessarily in a stand out role such as

---

[46] David Hathaway, 2004, *The Power of Faith*, pp. 47, 173. He goes on to add: *"God uses men. But only men and women willing to yield to His authority. I am not a big man with a little God. I am a little man with a big God! I may be a little David with a Goliath of a problem, but with my God I can..."* (p.48).

leading people to the Lord in big campaigns, preaching from the pulpit; an elder in the church or whatever. Well done you for carrying out and faithfully fulfilling your part, time and time again over the years. You did your bit, serving your Maker with commitment, dedication, sacrifice and love. You can look forward to our Lord taking you in His arms and saying: "Well done, good and faithful servant!" (Mt.25:23).

But maybe you're someone who lacks confidence and belief in yourself. Maybe, like me, you're not the extrovert type. Maybe you doubt your own ability (I managed 5 out of 40 in my first Old Testament test at Bible College, a whacking 12½ %!)[47]. Maybe, like the older Moses, you've lost your confidence and have doubts about your gifting and age, including your ability to lead, to be persuasive, forceful and to speak well (Ex.4:10, 6:12, 30).[48] Do you feel small "in your own eyes?" (1 Sam.15:17). Do you feel that you're not good enough? (1 Sam.18:18, 2 Sam.7:18). Maybe you don't know what your gift is. Well let me tell you this. God takes pity on the weak and needy (Ps.72:13). He uses the weak to shame the strong (1 Cor.1:27). His power is made perfect in weakness (2 Cor.12:9). Remember Paul's words in Philippians 4:13:

I can do everything through him who gives me strength.

Paul did not preach to the church in Corinth with eloquence or superior wisdom. Instead he came to them in weakness and fear and with much trembling (1 Cor.2:1-5). He also talks about his "thorn in the flesh" which was a heavy burden to him, so much so that he

---

[47] I would go on to teach a course on The Pentateuch, the first five books of the Bible (also called the Torah). God is good!
[48] Stephen's speech to the Sanhedrin in Acts chapter 7 is interesting. He talks about Moses being "educated in all the wisdom of the Egyptians," and being "powerful in speech and action" (v.22). He seems to be a changed man though when God calls him, at the age of 80 (vv.23, 30), to go back to Egypt to free His people and to be their ruler and deliverer (vv. 34-35). Clearly his confidence is gone and he now doubts his own ability.

pleaded with the Lord three times to have it taken away (2 Cor.12:7-10). While we don't know exactly what this was, many scholars believe it was some sort of problem with the eyes. (He mistakenly insulted the high priest, claiming afterwards that he did not realise who he was talking to. Yet Paul had been a Pharisee, thoroughly trained in the law under Gamaliel, as is stated in Acts 22:1-3, 23:2-6; cf. also Gal.4:15). Others suggest it was some sort of facial disfigurement which was "a trial" to the people (Gal.4:13-14), or malaria or other diseases. Whatever the thorn was, it caused Paul a lot of anxiety and torment.

Tradition portrays Paul as a physically small man who endured enormous physical hardships, threats and attacks on his life (2 Cor.11:23-33). Yet despite all this, God used him mightily for the furtherance and advancement of the Gospel. He went on to become one of the most influential early Christian missionaries, making three long journeys throughout the Roman Empire, evangelising everywhere he went, planting churches, appointing elders, performing many extraordinary miracles (Act.14:8-10, 19:11-12, 20:7-12, 28:8-9 etc.). His pastoral ministry was first rate as well as we read time and time again in the book of Acts. Both Paul and Barnabas strengthened the disciples, encouraging them to remain true to the faith (14:22, 16:5, 18:23, 20:2.) He was totally committed to them, a real people's person, visiting and revisiting the churches and in some cases, such as at Antioch, Corinth and Ephesus, spending longer periods of time with the brethren (14:28, 18:11, 19:10).

This was total commitment, a life dedicated to the service of the Lord and to the service of God's people. A man who was, in his own words, "ready...to die...for the name of the Lord Jesus" (21:13). Is it any wonder someone describes him as being "one of the greatest religious leaders of all time."

And what about Paul's writings? We haven't mentioned the fact that almost half of the books of the New Testament are accredited to his authorship (possibly 13 of the 27 books). He was undoubtedly a prolific writer, had a brilliant mind with a commanding knowledge of philosophy, religion and the Scriptures, and the ability to debate with the most educated scholars and Rabbis of his day. His clear, understandable explanation of the Gospel made his letters to the early churches the foundation of Christian theology, providing guidance, insight, understanding and so, so much more for Christians then and ever since. What a blessing this man has been. What a man! What a wee man! What an example for us to follow. His perseverance in the face of danger and persecution is an inspiration to us all. His attitude was incredible, being able to accept all his weaknesses, even boasting and delighting in them for the glory of God. He came to realise the power and strength that came from being weak (2 Cor.12:9-10)! We too need to persevere and keep on going, despite our hardships. We need to keep the faith and to persist and overcome our present difficulties, our doubts, our fears. We must never give up. We need to be totally dedicated and committed to the service of the Lord and to the service of God's people. We need to fight the good fight and finish the race. We too need to boast and delight in our weaknesses. For when we do, Christ's power rests on us and works through us (2 Cor.12:9).

Remember also Gideon, from the weakest clan and the least in his family. Look at how God used him! In the hands of God, his weakness was turned to strength:

I do not have time to tell you about Gideon, Barak, Samson, Jephthah, David, Samuel and the prophets, who through faith conquered kingdoms, administered justice, and gained what was promised; who shut the mouths of lions, quenched the fury of the flames, and escaped the edge of the sword; whose weakness was turned to strength; and who became powerful in battle and routed foreign armies (Heb.11:32-34).

They all were empowered and enabled. Their weaknesses were turned to strength. With the Lord on their side, victory was inevitable! The same God who enabled Moses, Gideon, David, Jonathan, William Carey and countless others, will enable us too. Don't doubt your ability as Moses and Jeremiah did (Jer.1:6). Don't think you're unimpressive like Gideon. Don't let anything hold you back because of your age (the youthful David,[49]) personality, gender, race, physical ability or whatever. In God's economy, there is no such thing as an insignificant person, an unimportant Christian. Every one of us has a role to play for Him and for His kingdom. God can use you too, to achieve things, to serve Him. You are unique! You are special! You are "God's workmanship, created in Christ Jesus to do good works" (Eph.2:10).

Remember John Haley, someone who gave his all, offering his body as a living sacrifice, holy and pleasing to God? Be like John! Find out what your gift is. Ask your Pastor or leaders or a good Christian friend who you respect and admire. There is a special niche for you to fill, a special ministry, a special task to fulfil. God has a purpose for you. Offer your services to a group in the church or at a local charity. Perhaps you've never played an instrument in a service or had the confidence to sing in the church choir or worship group, yet sing so beautifully in your own home. Perhaps you've never given your testimony in public or led a meeting. Perhaps you've never preached before or allowed your name to go forward to become a member of a particular committee or to take up a leadership position

---

[49] The phrase "only a little/child" is used to describe both Solomon and Jeremiah (1 Kg.3:7, Jer.1:6). David also describes his son as being "young and inexperienced" (1 Ch.22:5). Yet God was able to use these two men mightily; Solomon to be king and build the great temple, and Jeremiah to become one of the major prophets in Judah.

such as Treasurer, Secretary or whatever. Perhaps you've never witnessed to someone or led a person to the Lord. I don't know what your niche is. But God does. Ask Him to help you be and do what He wants.

There is no greater calling, no greater purpose in life than to serve our risen Lord, giving our all to Him. You have so much to offer. Believe in yourself. Believe in the gifting and empowering of the Holy Spirit. Believe in the helping hand of God that is always present with us. (Repeat again and again His declaration to us: "I will help you...I myself will help you," Is.41:13-14). Be amazed at the incredible things you will achieve for God.

I once heard about a missionary who served in Ethiopia at a very dangerous and difficult time. She had to constantly travel through a bandit infested area, risking her life in the process. "Aren't you scared of getting killed?" someone asked. Her reply was remarkable: "I died for the Lord ten years ago." What an attitude, willing to sacrifice even her life, for her Saviour and Lord! Her relationship with Him was on another level!

You've read about my journey; let Him continue to take you on yours. Open yourself up to God; to His greatness, to His magnificence, to His glory, and to His Presence (like the pillar of cloud and fire guiding the Israelites as they crossed the Red Sea). Let Him lead you each day. Let Him guide and speak to you. Listen out for His word, for that still, small, gentle whisper.

And dear reader, if you're not a Christian, let me encourage you too, to take that step of faith, in this instance by accepting Jesus as your personal Saviour. You too have fears and problems and stressful situations just like all of us. But you too can have that divine help in your life as well, if you take that step to become a Christian. I know it isn't easy; you can, in some cases, be subjected to ridicule and pressure, or even worse.[50] But it's the greatest decision you will ever make; to confess your sins to God, to turn to Him with tears of repentance and to invite Jesus into your heart. Do it now![51] Speak to a Christian friend and let them come and pray with you. Or get in touch with a local evangelical church. Take that step forward that will transform your life, enabling you to cope with all of life's problems and difficulties. Cross over from darkness to light. Enter into the kingdom of God, enjoying all the privileges that brings (as highlighted throughout the book). Rejoice, just like the angels in heaven (Lk.15:7, 10), at the change and transformation that will come over you. May God bless you and be with you. The grace of our Lord Jesus Christ be with you always.

And dear reader, if you once knew the Lord but have fallen away from Him, I want to encourage you to restore your relationship with the living God. Do not be like the church in Ephesus who had forsaken their first love. John implores them to:

Repent and do the things you did at first (Rev.2:4-5).

We all sin, as 1 John 1:8 makes clear. But we must not be controlled by sin, or "identified by a life of sin."[52] Instead, we should live a

---

[50] In some countries, new Christians are removed from the family, facing discrimination, poverty and persecution. For more information on the persecuted church worldwide, please contact Open Doors. In my case, it was only gentle ridicule at the traditional Boxing Day rugby match between Dungannon and Ballymena in Northern Ireland. On a packed side line, my mate turned round and, at the top of his voice shouted: "So Mark, I hear you've become a Christian!"

[51] I once heard a preacher share about an "impulse" he had to visit a member of his congregation in hospital. It turned out that there were two patients in the hospital with the same name, and the receptionist directed the minister to the wrong man! The man, who wasn't a Christian, was very poorly. That night, on his deathbed, he gave his life to Christ. The minister decided to return the next day to see how the man was progressing. But he had died overnight. Thankfully, at the last hour, he had come to know the Lord.

[52] www.gotquestions.org/backsliding-Christian.html

progressively more holy life as we grow closer to Christ.[53] What about you dear brother, dear sister? Have you turned away from God to pursue your own desires? Has something in this book hit a nerve, made you feel uncomfortable or moved you in some way? If this is the case, God is speaking to you, directly. He is telling you that you need to come back to Him - now. No matter what you have done, He promises to forgive:

"I will heal their waywardness and love them freely, for my anger has turned away from them" (Hos. 14:4).

If we confess our sins, he is faithful and just and will forgive us our sins and purify us from all unrighteousness (1 Jn. 1:9).

God loves you. He will welcome you back with open arms. Just like in the parable of the prodigal son, there will be much celebration and rejoicing:

But we had to celebrate and be glad, because this brother of yours was dead and is alive again; he was lost and is found (Lk. 15:32).

ETERNAL LIFE

I want to finish on a high note and, for the Christian, there is nothing more uplifting, more encouraging, more reassuring than the guarantee of eternal life. We are always planning for the future; working hard, paying off the mortgage, opening up savings accounts, contributing to a work pension, even preparing a will. It's a normal thing to do, making us feel secure, giving us peace of mind. With all these preparations we feel we've done our best to provide for ourselves and our family for the future. But the Bible talks about an

---

[53] Ibid

inheritance that is so much better than any amount of money or property we may have on earth. It talks about a home that will never crumble or be taken away. It talks about a life in the future that is guaranteed to last for ever, an inheritance that is promised to every child of God. Eternal life; the great Christian promise, the great Christian hope:

"For God so loved the world that he gave his one and only Son, that whoever believes in him shall not perish but have eternal life" Jn.3:16.

"Whoever believes in the Son has eternal life, but whoever rejects the Son will not see life, for God's wrath remains on him" Jn.3:36.

Jesus said to her, "I am the resurrection and the life. He who believes in me will live, even though he dies; and whoever lives and believes in me will never die" Jn.11:25-26.

"Do not let your hearts be troubled. Trust in God; trust also in me. In my Father's house are many rooms; if it were not so, I would have told you. I am going there to prepare a place for you. And if I go and prepare a place for you, I will come back and take you to be with me that you also may be where I am" Jn.14:1-3.

We had some Peruvian friends visit us recently who asked if it was possible to visit the National Wallace Monument, close to Stirling. The brochure states that this "is a place where history is something you can touch and feel, as you trace the story of Sir William Wallace, patriot, martyr, and Guardian of Scotland." The main attraction is definitely the high tower with 246 steps to the top! There is only one narrow stairwell making it quite awkward when other people are descending. But it is so worth battling on to get to the upper part with the fabulous views of Ben Lomond and the Trossachs to the west, the Pentland Hills to the east, not forgetting the River Forth, the city of

Stirling (and her beautiful castle), and the Ochil Hills. The top of the monument is actually called "The Crown," created by Victorian craftsmen on the Abbey Craig in the 1860's.

On a previous visit, one of our colleagues almost didn't make it to the top, the steps seeming to go on interminably, never ending, "continuous as the stars that shine and twinkle on the Milky Way".[54] With a bit of encouragement, however, she plodded on and was overjoyed to reach the crown. Sometimes we too have to plod on determinately, despite life's hardships, to reach our final destination, heaven. There we will be crowned in glory and righteousness by the great King Himself, reigning in victory and in His presence forever and ever (1 Pet.5:4, 2 Tim.4:8, 1 Cor.9:25). There we will receive the crown of life that God has promised to those who love Him (Jam.1:12, Rev.2:10).

The incredible news for us is that, spiritually speaking, everything is already sorted. Our futures are secure. God has anointed us, setting His seal of ownership on us, putting "his Spirit in our hearts as a deposit, guaranteeing what is to come" (2 Cor.1:21-22). The Holy Spirit "is a deposit guaranteeing our inheritance" (Eph.1:14). For make no mistake about it, heaven is where total perfection and bliss abound:

It is a place full of God's glory:

The Holy City...shone with the glory of God...The city does not need the sun or the moon to shine on it, for the glory of God gives it light, and the Lamb is its lamp (Rev.21).

---

[54] From William Wordsworth's poem, *"Daffodils."* The steps seemed to go on and on, just like the water from the Great Lakes, flowing continuously, never ending, over the mighty Niagara Falls!

In the Old Testament, when the glory of the Lord filled the temple of God, the priests were unable to perform their service (2 Chron.5:14). When Moses asked God in Exodus 33 to show him His glory, the Lord said:

"I will cause all my goodness to pass in front of you, and I will proclaim my name, the Lord, in your presence. I will have mercy on whom I will have mercy, and I will have compassion on whom I will have compassion. But, " he said, "you cannot see my face, for no-one may see me and live" (Ex.33:19-20).

But we will:

They will see his face, and his name will be on their foreheads. There will be no more night. They will not need the light of a lamp or the light of the sun, for the Lord God will give them light. And they will reign for ever and ever (Rev.22:4-5).

In the heavenly city, we will live as one with the King, living "*continually* in the atmosphere of the glory of God." [55] God will dwell with us personally:

"Now the dwelling of God is with men, and he will live with them. They will be his people, and God himself will be with them and be their God" (Rev.21:3).

Heaven is also a place of great joy. From time to time we experience moments of great joy and happiness. But they are only moments. Sadly, they do not last. Away from my family and Christian life, I can remember a time of immense joy, when visiting a place called Monkey Mia in Australia.[56] It is located in Shark Bay, Western Australia,

---

[55] So Grudem, ibid, P.1164.
[56] It actually has nothing to do with monkeys! The origin of the name is uncertain; it is perhaps connected to a schooner called "Monkey," anchored in the bay in 1834, along with the Aboriginal word "mia" for house or home, hence "home of the Monkey."

about 9 hours drive from Perth. More than 2000 dolphins and 28 shark species inhabit the Bay so, as you might expect, it is famous for its wild dolphins experience and is renowned as being one of the best places in the world for dolphin interaction. They say it's perfectly safe to swim and enjoy the turquoise water. Not so sure about that, but it's definitely **the place** to see dolphins up close in their natural habitat.[57] Today, this attraction draws over 100,000 people to the beach every year. Thankfully, it was relatively unknown when I visited in 1986 and was able to feed and touch them in relative peace and quiet. One hour later however, in the stifling heat of the outback (30°C plus 100% humidity), our old Holden panel van got a puncture. The feeling of peace and tranquillity from the visit to Monkey Mia was soon forgotten!

Not so with heaven! In the Holy City our joy will be multiplied many, many times over. Our joy, our happiness, our pleasure will last for ever. It will go on and on:

He will wipe every tear from their eyes. There will be no more death or mourning or crying or pain, for the old order of things has passed away (Rev.21:4).

"When we look into the face of our Lord and he looks back at us with infinite love," writes Grudem, "we will see in him the fulfilment of everything that we know to be good and right and desirable in the universe. In the face of God we will see the fulfilment of all the longing we have ever had to know perfect love, peace, and joy, and to know truth and justice, holiness and wisdom, goodness and power,

---

[57] At a remote headland in Cape Tribulation (a beautiful ecotourism centre, north of Cairns in northeast Queensland, Australia), I actually did swim with sharks close by! A tour was offered to one of the small neighbouring islands on the Great Barrier Reef. What an experience to snorkel in the pristine, blue waters; observing the incredible colours of the coral and the fish. And of the sharks! Thankfully, they were not the dangerous type, and there was plenty of other food on the menu for them!

and glory and beauty. As we gaze into the face of our Lord, we will know more fully than ever before that *"in your presence there is fullness of joy, at your right hand are pleasures for evermore"* (Psm.16:11). Then will be fulfilled the longing of our hearts with which we have cried out in the past, "One thing I have asked of the Lord, that will I seek after; that I may dwell in the house of the Lord all the days of my life, *to behold the beauty of the Lord,* and to inquire in his temple" (Psm.27:40).

"When we finally see the Lord face to face," continues Grudem, "our hearts will want nothing else: *...there is nothing upon earth that I desire besides you...God is the strength of my heart and my portion forever (*Psm.73:25-26). Then with joy our hearts and voices will join with the redeemed from all ages and with the mighty armies of heaven singing, *"Holy, holy, holy, is the Lord God Almighty, who was and is and is to come!"* (Rev.4:8).[58]

Where we are going to is a place of incredible beauty, compared by John to "a bride beautifully dressed for her husband" (Rev.21:2). He adds that "its brilliance was like that of a very precious jewel" (v.11), its wall made out of jasper, "and the city of pure gold, as pure as glass." Even the foundations are magnificent, "decorated with every kind of precious stone," jasper, sapphire, emerald, topaz, amethyst etc. (vv. 18-20). The 12 gates are made of pearls; the great street of pure gold. What a place; so beautiful, so rich, a place of extreme magnificence and splendour.

In the same way, we can also say that it is a place of total abundance:

On each side of the river stood the tree of life, bearing twelve crops of fruit, yielding its fruit every month (Rev.22:2).

---

[58] Grudem, Idid, p.1164.

Most farmers look forward to receiving one good harvest a year, or at the best, two. But 12? Not a chance! This language, a typical feature associated with the genre of apocalyptic literature, points to the truth or reality that lies behind the metaphor, which in this case is that heaven is a place of immense abundance.

As we walk along our life-paths, holding His hand, we are in touch with heaven. We find many hints along the way, experiencing touches of God's glory all around us. There are the rays of sunshine, originating from above, which provide warmth, good health and growth to the world, a bit like the Light that shines within our hearts. There are the early mornings, with the birdsong ringing out and the flowers opening their petals, the rivers and trees clapping their hands, the mountains and hills singing together for joy before the Lord (Ps.98:8-9, Is.55:12), all resonating praise to the King of kings and Lord of lords. Nature is alive with God's presence. Listen carefully for it. Look out for it. And His divine Presence lives within us too, in the form of the Holy Spirit. We have been imparted with new spiritual life. We have been "born of God." We have been brought to God. But the journey goes on, with the final destination heaven itself. The absolute certainty of our heavenly home gives us peace and joy. Let the hope of heaven encourage us today as we continue our walk along the path of life.

Eternal life offers the Christian immortality in the presence of God. It signifies the complete absence of physical and spiritual want, offering instead a life full of abundance and perfection that will last for ever. It means belongingness to God, which implies divine ownership and divine citizenship. It is a theme of great joy and happiness. No longer will there be death or mourning or crying or pain. The old age will pass away, being replaced by the New Jerusalem established in all its glory.

I hope this book has encouraged you and brought you closer to our Lord. It certainly has done that to me, bringing great blessing and anointing throughout the whole research and writing process. In fact, it started out as a sermon I was preparing, taking advantage of time at hand during lockdown. Then that incredible leading of the Holy Spirit! It quickly mushroomed into the book.

I want to finish with two things; an illustration I remember from Bible College, when visiting a church in Eyemouth, in the Scottish Borders. This will be followed by the words of one of my favourite songs, written by Paul Oakley. Be sure to watch it on You Tube!

May the Lord bless you richly as you continue your journey. *¡Amén, estimado hermano/a!* So be it, dear brother! Let it be so, dear sister, dear child of God!

"I am the Lord your God, who teaches you what is best for you, who directs you in the way you should go... He who has compassion on them will guide them and lead them beside springs of water... The Lord will guide you always; he will satisfy your needs in a sun-scorched land and will strengthen your frame" (Is.48:17, 49:10, 58:11).

EYEMOUTH ILLUSTRATION

A missionary couple were returning home by boat after over 35 years of dedicated service to the Lord, in very difficult circumstances and living conditions. They could only afford third class accommodation, but were able see the first class passengers above dressed in their beautiful outfits, smell the exotic food, hear the laughter. When they arrived at the port a large crowd had gathered to welcome the special travellers home. A band played at the ship's berth. A spacious, red carpeted gangway was put in place for disembarkation, for the first class passengers. The third class folk, however, had to almost fight their way out. The band was not playing to welcome the missionaries home. There was actually nobody there to greet them. In a moment of desperation, the husband blurted out, saying: "It's not fair. It's just not fair!" His wife, using the wisdom that women possess, turned her head to him and said gently: "We have not received a welcome Darling, because we're not home yet."

BECAUSE OF YOU

There's a place where the streets shine with the glory of the Lamb.

There's a way, we can go there, we can live there beyond time.

Because of You, because of You,

Because of Your Love,

Because of Your blood.

No more pain, no more sadness, no more suffering, no more tears.

No more sin, no more sickness, no injustice, no more death.

Chorus +All our sins are washed away, and we can live forever, now we have this hope, because of You.

Oh, we'll see you face to face, and we will dance together in the city of our God, because of You.

There is joy everlasting, there is gladness, there is peace.

There is wine, overflowing, there's a wedding, there's a feast.

Full chorus.